# Finding Democracy

## Through the Lens of Young German Woman, 1944-1950

by

Margaret F. Merritt, Ph.D.

RDS Publications
Fairbanks, Alaska

*Published by*
RDS Publications
Fairbanks, Alaska USA
rdspublications@gmail.com

Copyright © 2025 by Margaret F. Merritt

All rights reserved. No part of this publication may be reproduced without permission in writing from the publisher.

Library of Congress Control Number: 2025921634

Library of Congress Cataloging in Publication Data:
Merritt, Margaret F. 2025
    Finding Democracy Through the Lens of a Young German Woman, 1944-1950
    Includes references and original images

    1. Escape to an Uncertain Future 2. Among a Sea of Migrants 3. Finding Relief in Freising 4. Embracing A Democratic Life 5. New Friendships 6. Charting a Different Path

Printed in the United States of America

ISBN 978-0-9828392-9-4

For Tilly and her family

Remembering all young women caught in the traumas of war. May they survive perils, find ways to cope with suffering, and be given opportunities to pursue a hopeful future.

# Contents

|  | Page |
|---|---|
| *Preface* | vii |
| *Introduction* | ix |
| *Acknowledgments* | xiii |
| *Prologue* | xv |
|  |  |
| Part I Forced Decisions | 1 |
| Chapter 1. Escape to an Uncertain Future | 1 |
| Chapter 2. Among a Sea of Migrants | 13 |
|  |  |
| Part II Conquered Haven | 23 |
| Chapter 3. Finding Relief in Freising | 23 |
| Chapter 4. Embracing a Democratic Life | 43 |
|  |  |
| Part III Shifted Alliances | 61 |
| Chapter 5. New Friendships | 61 |
| Chapter 6. Charting a Different Path | 83 |
|  |  |
| *References and Notes* | 107 |
| *English Meaning of German Words* | 135 |
| *Index* | 139 |
| *Questions and Topics for Discussion* | 151 |

# *Preface*

My discovery of a cache of photo albums, pencil sketches, letters, personal notes, and various documents belonging to a young German woman was laid aside for many years while I navigated a busy life. The material covers the last gasps of Nazi Germany and the beginning of the American occupation, from 1944 to 1950. The importance of this unique inheritance from World War II and the postwar period did not crystallize in meaning until recent world events prompted my memory, and I pulled it out of storage for a closer look. When I realized the historical significance and relevance of the material, as well as the urgent declarations of people long dead, I began to research the history of the war and the forces that influenced civilians and combatants. I needed to place the material in context to unravel the story of this young woman who diligently chronicled her life journey during those pivotal years. I felt a responsibility to bring forth her memories from eighty years ago, because without reminders, past tragedies can be repeated.

The young woman's name was Tilly Keilitz. Of the 555 photos in her four albums, I selected eighty-eight to include in this book, along with two of her pencil sketches. These original images are augmented by maps, diagrams, and photos retrieved from declassified U.S. military archives.

After Tilly survived the war, she was employed by three U.S. Army organizations in Freising, a small Bavarian town outside Munich: the U.S. Army's Agricultural and Technical School for soldiers at Weihenstephan, the Freising Detachment of the 3rd Military Government Regiment, and the 604th Tactical Control Squadron. This book presents a unique portrayal of the interactions between Tilly, the American occupiers, and the residents of Freising as they navigated daily relationships that transformed their attitudes toward one another.

I built a story of actual events from Tilly's cache of material, as well as from more than seventy other sources, including academic documents about World War II warfare and U.S. military policy, Nazi politics, German life in the Third Reich including the postwar period, technical articles about army radar, aircraft, and bombs, lived experiences published by soldiers and refugees, U.S. Army archives, oral histories, and several papers translated from German. An overseas trip to tour Freising and meet with the city's archivist enriched my research. To bridge the gaps in writing about the past, I imagined some intimate scenes.

This book is not an exhaustive review or analysis of the period; neither does it pass moral judgment on the people mentioned. Instead, it offers a glimpse into a war-torn past through the perspective of a courageous young German woman as she discovers that her path to a brighter future lies in her embrace of an American democratic life.

# *Introduction*

Many narratives shape our understanding of history, each with a subtle perspective that adds clarity to past experiences. History is not just a fixed set of dates and events that add up to a known reality. Instead, history evolves as new information emerges and fresh interests develop. Different outlooks on the same situation can reveal startling truths and highlight the importance of careful handling and interpretation of information to avoid misconceptions. Every generation has the chance to discover and reexamine the lessons of history, and it is up to each of us to decide what lessons we will learn.

While much has been written about the Nazi state and the Allied war response, and autobiographies recount stories from soldiers, survivors, and expellees, it is rare to find an in-depth picture of American occupation forces from the viewpoint of a young German woman. Her perspective offers insights into how American officers influenced her understanding of freedom and democratic life after experiencing Nazi fascism. Tilly's personal story contributes to the German and American social histories of transitional wartime by bringing new images, descriptions, and documents to light. Her chronicle provides a glimpse into what life was like in 1940s Germany and how people coped with the difficult circumstances surrounding them.

This is a story about the struggle of a young German woman to survive the catastrophic end to her known world and redefine her identity. Although Germany had experimented with democracy during the Weimar Republic (1919–1933), numerous challenges weakened this short-lived republic, leading to the rise of Nazi fascism. As western Allied occupation forces prepared to reconstruct German political life along democratic lines, they found few survivors of pre-Nazi political parties. Consequently, they assumed that the German people needed to "learn" about democracy.[1] The U.S. occupation forces exposed the German populace to the American view of democracy. For young people in Tilly's generation, this was a time of inquiry into the concept of freedom.

Tilly's story is intersected by several themes: war, hunger, coming-of-age, and the relationship between photography and Tilly's evolving focus on her surroundings. World War II was the catalyst for this story. Its terrible history is relevant today because wars continue to create refugees and suffering. Rather than consign that unbearable time to vague recollections, we need to keep the bitter facts of history alive to avoid repeating our past mistakes. For those who are fortunate to have never experienced war, stories like the one described in this book provide a glimpse of what it might have been like. The war deepened Tilly's desire to feel intensely and to savor life. It brought her together with people she would otherwise never have met, and these relationships changed her destiny. By revealing Tilly's experiences and detailing the work of American military servicemen and German public servants determined to rebuild a devastated society, this story illuminates the human spirit's capacity to persevere and seek an optimistic future.

Hunger caused by food shortage pervades this story. The scarcity of food for Aryan Germans was Hitler's rationale for plunder and was of great importance in the Nazi war strategy. Hunger fueled the black market, and the suffering caused by hunger drove millions to migrate in the aftermath of war. Staving off starvation was a critical component in the Allied mission to rebuild a self-governing Germany politically reformed along democratic lines because empty-bellied Germans had little interest in politics. Repeated German crop failures tested American resolve, policy, and actions to feed a vanquished nation. The Soviet Union's attempt to consolidate Berlin under their economic control through a blockade prompted the Allies to undertake a massive humanitarian airlift, thereby transforming conquerors into saviors. I cannot overstate how vital the production and acquisition of food was as a weapon of war and an instrument of peace.

Tilly's records not only provide a unique occupation narrative but also enhance the history of women by reporting on her adaptations to frightening changes in her world. She is not portrayed as a heroine; neither is she a victim. Like her, everybody suffered and lost something—she represents the young woman who seeks to survive war and control her fate. Despite attempts to direct her beliefs through mandatory participation in Nazi youth programs, she rejected their oppressive ideology and sought a new beginning during the American occupation with an emerging sense of freedom. She came of age while employed by the occupation forces and, through their influence, came to embrace American democratic ideals.

Her transition into womanhood parallels Germany's transformation into a different society. Tilly and her nation persevered through challenges, confronted a reprehensible past, and found hope in new possibilities through American policy, actions, and cultural exchange. The relationships with American occupation forces and demonstrations of empathy toward the plight of German people, convinced many Germans to align their vision with that of the Americans, thus restoring Germany into a democratic republic and an important ally.

Using drawing paper and pencils or a camera, Tilly chronicled the world around her; she amassed a visual record of enjoyable memories, postwar trauma, places to which she felt a deep connection, and the men and women she passed her time with. Many images depict the quiet moments of people as they sought relief from stress through fellowship and play. These behind-the-scenes views bring nuance to the postwar account of American servicemen and their relationships with residents. Tilly's photography became more sophisticated as she matured, increased her skills, and benefited from advancements in camera technology. In 1944, her photos taken with the Agfa Box camera reflect her personal priorities. By 1946, her photos with the more advanced Rolleicord camera indicate a shift in her focus to a broader examination of events, suggesting a more thoughtful perspective.

The book is organized into three parts. Part I, "Forced Decisions," details Tilly's strategies for survival during the last days of Nazi Germany from 1944 to 1945. Part II, "Conquered Haven," describes the American occupation of Freising from 1945 to 1946 and Tilly's embrace of American democratic ideals. Part III, "Shifted Alliances," relates the adjustments of Tilly, West Germany, and the Americans to challenges emerging in the postwar period of 1946 to 1950.

# *Acknowledgments*

I treasure and feel humbled by the war memories shared by Christel Rosenberg. I understand that her memories of hunger and the loss of security were painful, and I am grateful for her willingness to share them with me. Because of her, I could better portray the harsh realities inflicted on German civilians by the combatants of World War II.

I am indebted to Assistant Professor for German Language, Helga Wagenleiter, M.A., M.A.Ed., for her contributions to this book. She asked insightful questions, suggested alternative interpretations of policies and events from a German perspective, and made improvements throughout the manuscript.

Many thanks are due to Dr. des. Isabella Hödl-Notter, historical researcher, Germany, who clarified several details regarding Freising that are presented in this book and provided valuable references for my research. I have enjoyed corresponding with Isabella about Freising's history.

My thanks to Stephanie Kuchinke, Archivist, Stadtarchiv Freising, for her guided tour of locations in Freising, including houses on Ganzenmullerstraße, the *Rathaus* at Marienplatz, St. George's Parish Church, and site of the former Vimy barracks. Ms. Kuchinke's explanations of the area's history contributed to my better understanding of Freising.

I greatly appreciate Cathy Lair's early review, cheerful support, and encouragement. I am grateful to Major Kenneth

C. Grenier, retired, U.S. Marine Corps, for identifying U.S. Army Air Corps fighter and bomber aircraft photos in this book and for examining my writings on aviation for their accuracy.

I am indebted to Jerry Brown, Archives Technician and Anti-terrorism Officer, Air Force Historical Research Agency at Maxwell Air Force Base, Alabama, for fulfilling my request to access declassified files of the 604th Tactical Control and Warning Squadron, 1946-1950. Thanks to the Hoover Institution Library and Archives at Stanford University for allowing access to their records on Office of Military Government for Bavaria, Freising, Field Operation Division.

# *Prologue*

*The Nazis entered this war under the rather childish delusion that they were going to bomb everyone else, and nobody was going to bomb them ... They sowed the wind, and now they are going to reap the whirlwind.* ~ Sir Arthur T. Harris

U.S. Army Air Forces (USAAF) Lieutenant General James H. "Jimmy" Doolittle, commander of the powerful 8th Air Force deployed in East Anglia, England, was outraged at the order he had just received from General Carl A. Spaatz, commander of the U.S. Strategic Air Forces in Europe. It was January 31, 1945, and the Allies had not yet achieved the annihilation of the Nazi regime, which had shaken world order and produced terror on an unprecedented scale. Spaatz had ordered an aerial assault on Berlin by the 8th Air Force on February 3, 1945.[1,2] To Doolittle, the order sounded a lot like the Americans were to bomb a city full of civilians, and this went against his principles. He believed the order betrayed the foundations of American morals and argued that the attack would "violate the basic American principle of precision bombing of targets of strictly military significance."[3] Spaatz told Doolittle to "shut the hell up."[4]

Overruling Doolittle's objections, Spaatz emphasized that the attack on Berlin was justified and of great political importance.[5,6] Legitimate targets lay within the city. Berlin was Hitler's capital and it included headquarters for the

Gestapo and Luftwaffe, industrial complexes, and an extensive railway system.[7] The February 3 attack aimed to aid the Soviet ground forces marching toward Berlin from the Vistula River in Poland. An aerial deathblow would save casualties among troops on the ground.

If any military organization could take on Berlin in 1945, it was the 8th Air Force—the largest air strike force ever assembled.[8] The attack force, consisting of 15,000 airmen in forty-two bombardment groups organized into three divisions, was scattered across seventy-one airfields in East Anglia.[9] The primary U.S. bombers used against Nazi Germany were the B-17 Flying Fortress and the B-24 Liberator.[10] Along with the Royal Air Force's Avro Lancaster, these Allied bombers had the distance and payload capacity needed for bombing campaigns deep into German territory.[11] American fighters, the P-47 Thunderbolt, the P-38 Lightning, and the P-51 Mustang, were assigned as escorts to the bombers.[12]

Their payloads were two types of bombs, explosive and incendiary. The 4,000-pound explosive bomb had enough force to make roofs fly off and knock out the doors and windows of houses located a kilometer away from the strike. The various gruesome incendiary devices included a mixture of gasoline, rubber, oil, liquid asphalt, and magnesium that created a synthetic lava; white phosphorus that burned in the air; and rags soaked in benzene. The best way to create a fast-moving wall of flame in an urban center was to drop explosive bombs to blow off roofs and doors, thus exposing the interior of the structures to subsequent attacks with incendiary bombs.[13]

Doolittle knew that Berlin was a difficult target to bomb. A large and sprawling imperial city of brick and stone, 891 square kilometers in area, the city was located 880 km from air bases in East Anglia and upon arrival, was heavily defended.[14] The German anti-aircraft defense system included deception, concealment, early warning,[15] nimble warplanes,[16] and highly lethal and effective anti-aircraft guns accompanied by searchlight batteries.[17,18]

On February 3, the 8th Air Force was sent on two missions. In the first, 1,003 B-17 bombers and 575 P-51 escort fighters were to bomb the Tempelhof marshalling yard in Berlin and conduct strikes on targets of opportunity in the city. Simultaneously, 434 B-24 bombers and 38 P-51 escort fighters were to hit the synthetic oil industry at Magdeburg, 160 km southwest of Berlin.[19]

In the predawn darkness, navigator-meteorologists with the 653rd squadron flew weather and reconnaissance assignments ahead of the combat mission. They reported that conditions over Berlin would be CAVU—ceiling and visibility unlimited. On cue, flares from control towers signaled pilots to start their engines, and the sound of 2,050 warplanes reverberated across East Anglia. The planes took off beginning at 0715 and took two hours to assemble into battle formation before crossing the North Sea, heading for the Dutch coast.[20] The endless procession of perfectly arranged bombers in a V formation, staggered in height and offset laterally, entering the Third Reich's airspace stretched for 580 km—it was "something beyond imagination."[21] The sheer number of American bombers cruising in perfect formation at 180 mph across German skies in broad daylight affirmed the opinion of many German people that the Nazi regime was doomed.[22]

The pilots never deviated from their assigned path, flying into the thick of the flak to complete their mission. For nearly two hours, the stream of bombers approached the capital city, made their target run, dropped tons of explosives near the smoking ruins inflicted by the preceding bomber, and returned to England. Postwar analysis revealed that in addition to the Tempelhof marshalling yard and its extensive system of rail lines, hundreds of buildings in the government sector were destroyed or badly damaged, including Gestapo and Air Ministry headquarters and the Reich Chancellery, forcing Hitler to move into his underground bunker.[23] An estimated 2,500 people died in the attack, and 100,000 homes were destroyed.[24]

# PART I
# Forced Decisions

## Chapter 1. Escape to an Uncertain Future

On February 3, 1945, the high whine of the siren pierced the air with insistent urgency, as it had many times before. Tilly and her coworkers at the Allgemeine Elektrizitäts Gesellschaft (AEG) Research Institute in Berlin raced to a small, windowless room situated between the back courtyard and the front office that served as the building's bomb shelter. She settled in a chair against a wall of the bomb shelter while her boss and a dozen other people found seats around the room. She heard muffled thunder as shells exploded in the distance and, while she waited for the danger to pass, pondered how she came to be in such circumstances.

\*\*\*

The previous fall, when she was nineteen years old, Tilly began work at AEG Research Institute in Berlin as a lab trainee in an apprenticeship program. Her aptitude in physics and chemistry in high school had qualified her for a job in one of the many research labs of AEG, a large and innovative producer of electronic equipment.[1] In addition to its research labs headquartered in Berlin, AEG produced electric consumer goods such as irons, toasters, and ovens at several factories throughout Europe.[2]

Intelligent and inquisitive, Tilly did not fit the patriarchal Nazi mission for women of the Third Reich to devote themselves entirely to family care at home. A prominent Nazi worldview or *Weltanschauung* promoted by Adolf Hitler, *Führer* of Germany's powerful Nazi Party, encouraged German women to embrace motherhood as a career and raise the Aryan birth rate through marriage.[3,4] While Tilly believed that raising a child could be deeply fulfilling, her mother, Grete, had nurtured in Tilly a determined spirit to choose her own path. She had a strong inner drive to improve herself and her financial condition, so when skilled labor was needed in industries to fill gaps left by men drafted into the war, Tilly welcomed the opportunity for professional achievement created by a shortage of men.

Exciting theoretical and experimental work occurred in AEG's Berlin research labs, including the invention of the first electron microscope. Applications of electron optics to chemistry, bacteriology, and medicine were ongoing investigations in the early 1940s.[5] In the division where Tilly worked, physicists and engineers had achieved advancements in sound recording equipment. In 1927, German engineer Fritz Pfleumer found that he could make magnetic tape by gluing iron oxide onto thin paper strips. In 1932, he sold his patent to AEG, which led to the development of the world's first tape recorder, the Magnetophon K1.[6]

When Hitler became the Chancellor of Germany in 1933, the Nazi Party seized control of the government and aggressively demanded ideological compliance of the people and industry. The directors of AEG responded to this threat by adding manufacturing lines to supply the Nazis' war effort, with some of these production lines eventually staffed with forced laborers.[7] However, Tilly had no idea what happened in AEG's factories hundreds of kilometers away from Berlin, and like most Berliners, her spare energy was spent on the struggle to survive bombing raids and fend off hunger.

The Allied large-scale carpet bombing of German infrastructure and homes designed to demoralize the German people and assist the Soviet offensive in the east regardless of civilian casualties had caused half the population of 4 million Berliners to flee the city. Those remaining had no wish to leave, nowhere to go, or were, like Tilly, assigned to industries. Tilly buried herself in work, determined to perform her duties well despite the constant physical and emotional hardships of growing up in a war zone.

Born in Berlin in 1925, Tilly's parents divorced when she was six. Tilly spent the next five years living with her mother and maternal grandparents in Vienna, where Grete earned money by selling whalebone corsets. In 1936, Grete remarried and returned to Berlin with twelve-year-old Tilly, where they lived with Tilly's new stepfather, Paul, who owned a pharmacy. Two years later, Tilly's sister, Christel, was born.

All German youth were to be educated in the spirit of National Socialism according to Nazi ideology. Membership in Hitlerjugend (for boys), and Bund deutscher Mädels (for girls), at age fourteen was decreed mandatory for Aryan youth.[8] Through misleading propaganda carefully crafted by Hitler's disinformation chief, Joseph Goebbels, and state-sponsored repressive tactics executed through Heinrich Himmler's Schutzstaffel (SS) organization, the Nazi regime attempted to direct Tilly's beliefs, values, and actions in ways that were compatible with the ideology of the Third Reich. Parents who failed to enroll their children in these official branches of the Hitler Youth movement were subject to heavy prison sentences while their children were whisked away to orphanages.

Membership in the Hitler Youth, however, did not mean support for the Nazis, who ruled through fear and relied on quiet complicity.[9] Germany was not united behind the Nazis, but an intelligence subdivision of the SS employed spies to report on any critical comments against the Nazi state. Whether people griped about long lines to buy food, shortages of household goods, or voiced doubts about the progress of the war, those who expressed negative feelings risked fines, imprisonment, or even death. The brutal police threats made people apprehensive about whispering their thoughts.[10]

Grete, a strong and independent-minded woman, was disgusted at the Nazi bureaucrats who sought to justify a war that starved her children, risked their safety, and left them to a grim future. She did not believe Hitler's assurances that the sufferings of the German people would be avenged by a wonder weapon—the V-2 rocket. In October 1944, their home in Berlin was bombed, destroying many beautiful Middle Eastern treasures and a baby grand piano Tilly had inherited from her late father.

During the winter of 1944–1945, Tilly's family was forced to find alternative housing in Berlin. They lived in precarious times—where a bomb fell could determine their fate. The repeated piercing whistle of falling bombs, wail of sirens, and rapid bursts of flak from anti-aircraft guns terrorized Tilly's little sister, causing her to vomit through sleepless nights. Grete knew that the Nazis could not protect her family, so she was preparing to take Christel away from Berlin by train to Austria, where they could stay with relatives.

Tilly's stomach rumbled, diverting her thoughts from her family's imminent departure to her hunger pangs. Sighing, she reminisced about her time as a farm laborer in the Reichsarbeitsdienst (RAD), a national labor program she had served in before her appointment at AEG. In 1943, at age eighteen, Tilly was conscripted into six months' service for the Third Reich, like all able-bodied high school graduates. The national labor program was divided into two sections: one for men and one for women. Tilly was assigned to work at two *Arbeitslagers*, or labor camps, Lager Hohenzollerndorf and Lager Giesebitz, in the province of Pomerania, northeast of Berlin. The labor camps accommodated ten to twenty young women who were assigned the task of food production.

At the labor camp, Tilly was grateful to escape Berlin's frequent bombing raids and have access to fresh eggs and milk, a rarity in the city. She became friends with the other young women as they worked in the fields, raking sheaves of grain into stacks to dry before the threshing, the air permeated with the earthy fragrance of ripened wheat. Her pals included Hilde, Lotte, Lia, Marianne, Edith, Hannelore, Elsbet, Hanne, and Ilse. As always, she had her sketch pad, pencils, and camera at hand to chronicle the world around her, amassing a visual record of her life, the lives of people she knew, and her surroundings. Her well-used Agfa Box 44 camera, lightweight and compact, accompanied her to the RAD work farms.[11] By capturing images of RAD girls in gay spirits while they worked for the common good of Germany, Tilly's labor camp supervisors granted the girls permission to use their cameras.

All the girls wore the same uniform in the field: a blue dress and white apron. The RAD service dress uniform was a white blouse with a brown wool jacket and skirt. A brooch was worn at the neck, adorned with the Nazi swastika above two barley spikes, signifying the provision of agricultural service to the Third Reich.

Tilly's sketch of *Arbeitsmädels* working, 1944.

From left: Lotte, Lia, Tilly, Marianne, Edith, Hannelore, and Elsbet, 1944.[12]

Folk dancing at Lager Hohenzollerndorf, 1944.

**Tilly in a RAD service dress uniform, 1944.**[13]

As an *Arbeitsmädel,* or female laborer, Tilly worked twelve hours a day, six days a week, for 0.20 Reichsmark a day.[14] She felt pride in her hard work and loved caring for the farm animals, but it was not all work. Sometimes, the girls practiced folk dancing, and there were fleeting moments to have fun and enjoy being carefree teenagers. On one holiday trip, the girls splashed in the waves of the Baltic Sea at Rügenwalde, two years before that German enclave was transferred to Poland following the defeat of Nazi Germany.

Tilly's help was needed to produce food at the labor camps because excessive rain and an early winter had diminished Germany's agricultural output, already depressed from a lack of nitrogen and phosphate fertilizers diverted into making bombs, the drafting of laborers, and the destruction of farmland by Allied bombs. As a result of the crop shortages and difficulties transporting produce via damaged railways, severe cuts to rations for bread, meat, and potatoes had been implemented.[15]

Food was of great importance in the Nazi ideology because it symbolized economic self-sufficiency—one of Hitler's primary justifications for conquest and control of more arable land for Germany. He vowed that never again must Germans suffer and die of starvation, as had thousands of them during World War I. In his quest for more *Lebensraum* or living space for Aryan Germans, Hitler had advocated to "Give soil for the German plow through the German sword, while giving the nation its daily bread."[16] Food shortages were an embarrassing admission of failed Nazi ambitions. Despite the ruthless redirection of food supplies from occupied countries to the homeland, daily rations for Germans living in cities dropped to less than half of what they were used to eating at the beginning of the war.[17]

Because shortages and rations made shopping difficult, Grete was anxious about what food she could put on the table at home. Although National Socialist planners promised to formulate food rations to treat everyone in the *Volksgemeinschaft* equally, these assurances were not fulfilled and the food situation did not improve. Grete had to register with a local shop, stand in a long line, hand over her daily ration card and money to the shop owner, and await whatever foodstuffs he would give her to attain the allocated calories. The family diet consisted primarily of potatoes or turnips, some beans or dried apples, and if they were lucky, a cheap cut of pork, cooked together in a single pot and thickened with a little flour. This spartan dish, called *Eintopf,* was promoted by Nazi propagandists as strengthening the German will to "discipline their hunger in the service of the war effort."[18]

Scarcity was deeply felt during the winter of 1944, and for those who could afford it, acquiring food on the black market became a part of everyday life. Tilly's family possessed few valuables to barter, and Grete did not want to risk arrest and imprisonment by violating the War Economy Regulation.[19] She coped with limited rations by eating the rotten parts of potatoes and giving Tilly and Christel the good bits. Six-year-old Christel was always hungry. One day, she saw a neighbor peeling a potato and begged the woman for a few scraps of peels. The woman refused to give her any, insisting she needed all the peels to make soup for her family, leaving a devastated Christel still hungry. Deteriorating conditions—food and coal shortages, spotty streetcar service, electricity blackouts—created an uneasiness in Berliners. There were growing rumors that the war was not going well.

\*\*\*

Tilly was jolted out of her reflections about the past by a thunderous explosion that struck the bomb shelter. Because AEG supplied essential materials for the German people as well as the Nazi war effort, its Berlin research lab was a logical target for the Allied bombers, and they had hit their mark. Thrown to the floor with force, she choked on the smoke that smelled of gunpowder mixed with fresh blood. She struggled to contain her fear of being buried alive. Years later, Tilly described the brutal shock of emerging from the aftermath of the bomb's direct hit on her building.

> This date will be engraved in my mind as long as I live. On February 3, 1945, the firm I worked in,

AEG, in the north of Berlin, was hit by two bombs—one in front and one in the courtyard. Our shelter was in between, and the walls just crumbled; heavy posts keeled over. We had several wounded and two dead. People I worked with. My boss got a beam on his foot and got that broken. A girl had a fist-sized hole in her calf. One man was lying with his head detached. I shook off the dust from the crumbled mortar and crawled out from under a hollow a fallen beam had made, unscathed. God must have thought it was not time for me yet. I helped the wounded boss out of the wreckage, then started the long trek home. It took three hours. Some trams were running, some buses, many kilometers on foot. And houses were burning on both sides of the streets. What inflames the minds of men and sets them against each other? I wish people who are frenzied to build more and more fancy weapons, poisons, and nuclear bombs would reflect on this incident and remember that next time there may be no getting out alive.

In the pale winter sun, Tilly stumbled through the rubble of once grand buildings. A world leader in science and art, the city was dotted with elegant museums, galleries, and theaters that now lay in the streets, their granite walls reduced to skeletal remains wrapped in acrid smoke. She watched people emerge from homes that had become charred shells of brick with roofs blown off, hastily putting out fires. She could feel the air being sucked in to feed the arching yellow flames. Those not busy battling fires frantically dug through smoking debris for lost loved ones or possessions. She couldn't tell which and didn't linger to ask. Dazed and weary, Tilly was determined to endure because there was nothing else to do; life must go on. She recalled, "When I finally reached home, my mother was white when she opened the door. She said my hair was white, too, from mortar dust."

The February 3 bombing of Berlin was the largest of air assaults that targeted the city. The concentrated shelling caused a wind-driven fire that burned eastward through the city for four days until it had consumed everything combustible in its path. The streets were blocked with rubble, snarling transportation, and large areas of Berlin were without electricity. Berliners struggled with water, food, and electricity shortages. They were tired of the thunder of artillery and the hail of bombs. They wanted the *Führer* to rot in Hell and the war to be over. Most of all, they wanted to survive the cataclysm of impending defeat.[20]

Rumors raced through the neighborhood that Russians were marching into Berlin from the east. People were afraid of the cruelty of the Russians, who were known to seize women and sack properties with no concern for the abuse they inflicted. In later years, Tilly haltingly recounted how Russian soldiers had captured one of her high school girlfriends and raped her, then killed her family. Her friend survived the gang rape but hanged herself.

Fearing for their safety, the family left Berlin in separate directions. Because pharmacists were deemed essential to the Nazi war effort, Paul was not allowed to close his pharmacy and leave the city, so he went to stay with an aunt who lived in a hamlet southwest of Berlin. Grete took Christel to the train station, where they squeezed into a carriage taking Wehrmacht reinforcements to Austria. Upon reaching Vienna, Grete was dismayed to discover that her parents had no spare food for them. Instead, Grete and Christel went to stay with friends of her mother's in the small town Mänk for the duration of the war. In the country, people could find something to eat.

Because bombs had destroyed their headquarters, AEG transferred Tilly's division to the small industrial town of Thalheim in the state of Saxony, 280 km south of Berlin. Her company assured Tilly that she would find food and safety in Thalheim, so she made plans to go there. Some of Tilly's coworkers were transferred to other divisions or were hired by different companies. Tilly recounted, "One of my colleagues at AEG was a pretty and very smart young woman named Helga Kühl. After damage made our lab inoperable, she was hired by the Peenemunde staff. We were so proud of her because only the smartest were employed there. She probably knew Wernher von Braun. I often wondered if she survived the war."

In the struggle for survival, people can be left with no good decisions. Tilly's resolve to flee possible death in Berlin from bombs or the Russians for an uncertain future was instinctive. She embarked on the journey to Thalheim, not knowing the risks that lay ahead.

## Chapter 2. Among a Sea of Migrants

After packing a small suitcase with a few worn and carefully mended clothes, Tilly slipped on a winter coat, stepped off her doorstep in Berlin, and set out on her journey to Thalheim. With few buses in operation, she had to find additional means of transportation. Truck drivers occasionally let her catch a ride for a few kilometers, and she was sometimes offered a lift on a horse-drawn cart.

In February 1945, Tilly was among the thousands of evacuees streaming into the countryside from cities, escaping large-scale bombardment and the dreaded Soviet invaders. The German government encouraged women with children and the aged to leave endangered cities for rural areas. The evacuees were seen on roads everywhere, carrying rucksacks on their backs or wheeling carts and wheelbarrows piled with belongings. This massive displacement of people worsened the already crowded conditions and food shortages.[1]

One day, as she walked through a village, the abrupt buffeting whine of fighter-bombers fast approaching, flying low, broke the calm of the morning. Fearing that they were Soviet pilots seeking ground targets to strafe, she ran. Suddenly, leaden bullets ricocheted off the cobblestones behind her, striking the ground so rapidly that they made an ear-splitting brrrt sound. Ducking and dodging, she ran hard as bullets slammed into stone walls lining the street. Then, the pilot pulled up and veered off, ending the storm of bullets. Miraculously, she was not hit, but the attack left her shaking with fright.

Tilly arrived in Thalheim in early March. Resting against the Erzgebirge Mountains separating Germany from Czechoslovakia, the town was just emerging from winter. She secured lodging and resumed her work as a laboratory technician for AEG. Meanwhile, Grete and Christel were adjusting to life as refugees in Lower Austria. Christel recalled that they had to sleep on straw in the attic of the grandmother's farmhouse, but at least there was enough food and no bombs.

In April 1945, the 83rd Armored Reconnaissance Battalion of the U.S. Army methodically swept through Saxony, eliminating Nazi resistance. They secured Thalheim on April 15.[2] American occupation of towns occurred as they were conquered, with military government detachments deployed as soon as possible to relieve the tactical troops. A similar process was repeated in countless towns: an American tank convoy moved into the town square to neutralize resistance, if there was any; the enemy commander and his men were rounded up and arrested; Allied flags were raised above the city hall or *Rathaus*; and the Germans were assembled to listen to their first orders by the victors.

> This town has surrendered unconditionally to Allied Forces. City Hall is designated as Headquarters, and you are under command of the Allied Military Government. No further resistance will be tolerated. All schools are closed. All legal and financial business

is suspended. All motor vehicles are requisitioned, and all stores and petrol are confiscated. The town is under a curfew from 1900 to 0600 daily and violators will be shot. All town officers will report to Allied Headquarters immediately and all civilians will return to their homes.[3]

Tilly was not surprised and felt relieved at the fall of Thalheim and neighboring German towns to the Americans. It was past time for the cursed war to end, and the Americans were preferred victors to the Russians, who were loathed for their cruelty. On May 7, the German High Command surrendered all land, sea, and air forces unconditionally to Allied forces. Following President Harry S. Truman's declaration of Victory in Europe (VE) Day on May 8, 1945, the AEG company was dissolved.

As the dust settled on the battlefield, the four Allied Powers returned all territories annexed by Germany to their respective countries and ceded parts of Pomerania, Silesia, and Prussia to Poland and the Soviet Union. Although only a few newspapers and radio stations intermittently broadcast news to the vanquished German people, Tilly had heard that the Allied powers had divided the shrunken country into four zones of occupation in a joint administration of governance. Eastern Germany went to Russia, regions west of the Rhine River were assigned to France, the British wanted the northwestern states, and the Americans were given central and southeastern states. Berlin was also divided into four zones of occupation.[4] All towns currently controlled by the U.S. Army outside the American zone boundaries would be handed over to the respective Allied authorities.

When the American forces in Thalheim were notified that the Soviets would move in, they didn't tarry. In dismay, Tilly watched the Americans prepare to leave. The Russians were 160 km north of Thalheim and marching resolutely south to secure their spoils of war—the occupation and exploitation of eastern Germany.[5] The imminent arrival of Russian troops in Thalheim and the very real prospect of an orgy of revenge inflicted by those victors on their defeated enemy gave Tilly no choice but to run from danger again and face difficult questions about how to ensure her safety and secure a means of livelihood.

\*\*\*

The sky was clear with a warm spring breeze as Tilly left Thalheim in May 1945, suitcase in hand, walking south. Her brisk pace slowed as the heat of the day and its accompanying hunger and thirst appeared. She planned to cross into Bavaria, where the Russians would not have authority. With the railways in ruins, the best route to the border between the Russian occupation zone of Saxony and the American occupation zone of Bavaria, 80 km from Thalheim, was following the small country pathways leading to Hof.

Tilly revealed, "Along the way, I met a wounded German soldier." As she listened to the young man's story, she noted the tension in his jaw and the hollows of his cheeks, pale with pain. The soldier, barely out of his teens, had crept away from the battlefield. Drafted unwillingly into the Wehrmacht, he had no interest in sacrificing any more of his life to the failed Nazi regime. He only wished to rejoin his parents in a small village just north of Munich. When he heard that Germany had surrendered, he ditched his stained uniform for civilian clothes to evade capture by the Allies. They were both alone and in need of support, so they formed a temporary alliance. Tilly recalled, "We helped each other, walking, or sometimes we got rides on a horse-drawn cart or a truck."

They passed out of the thick forests of the Erzgebirge, sheltering in the evening around a campfire in fallen barns, crumbled buildings, or open fields, and crossed into Bavaria. Upon reaching Hof, secured by the U.S. Army's 90th Division on April 16,[6] Tilly and her companion found a crowded reception in the damaged town. Hof had taken in refugees from neighboring Sudetenland, where the Czech government was conducting an extensive ethnic cleansing campaign against the German-speaking population. With its industries reprogrammed for war production by the Nazis, Hof had sustained heavy bombing a few months before their arrival. The Allies had destroyed over a hundred homes, which were now badly needed for unwanted refugees placing pressure on limited housing and food supplies.

As a postwar internally displaced person, Tilly joined a migrating sea of bewildered civilians, discarded slave laborers, defeated soldiers, expelled *Volksdeutsche*, and liberated prisoners of diverse nationalities. They streamed into roads on foot, with bicycles, riding horse-drawn wagons or pulling handcarts. Few trucks were in operation as gasoline was in short supply. Some people waited on congested railway platforms for irregularly running trains. Women, children, old men, and an occasional young man, whole and broken, determined and dazed, were all going somewhere. Tilly was wary of mingling with these homeless pilgrims. Many, like herself, were fleeing from the Russians, but she wondered at the varied languages, Dutch, French, and Polish, murmured by somber groups walking slowly north and westward. Someone explained that these were slave laborers, forced to work in Nazi factories, now freed by the Americans and searching for a way back to their home countries.

Resting in evening shadows after a long day of walking, Tilly sketched images of the people she had seen along the road, the effects of war's aftermath in their faces. A thin and bedraggled mother begged for food for her hungry children. A lean, hopeless man stood gazing in silence at nothing in particular. An old man with matted whiskers reluctantly asked for help. A young girl sat crumpled against a wall, hugging herself, irrevocably traumatized. Peace was here, but there was no joyous shouting. The people were quiet with sadness, their expressions serious or broken with tears. The scenes she witnessed were disturbing, and in the process of sketching, she released her distress. With each determined stroke of the pencil, she explored what she saw, confronting its reality yet exerting control over its shape and reflection. Her pencil reestablished a small sense of empowerment amid suffering and uncertainty.

**Tilly's sketches on the road, 1945.**

While Tilly grappled with the dawning realities of a Germany unfamiliar to her, Grete and Christel faced a much different fate. Declared independent from Nazi rule on April 27, 1945, Austria was divided, like Germany, into Allied zones of occupation. The Soviets quickly moved into Lower Austria and established a communist government ruled by the Kremlin. Red Army troops combed the countryside for plunder, and several Russians established themselves in the farmhouse where Grete and Christel were staying to feast on their meager food stores. As recalled by Christel, then just six years old, "Russian soldiers stayed in the farmhouse, too, below, while we stayed in the loft. We stayed there in farmhouses until May 1946, having not heard anything of my dad, who had remained in Berlin to protect his pharmacy."

Also sharing the road with the migrating Europeans were American soldiers in their jeeps. No longer combatants, the soldiers had transformed into a security force, patrolling to maintain order, stifle resistance, and enforce the laws of the rapidly emerging Offices of the Military Government, United States (OMGUS). Food was scarce. Knowing that the homeless needed to be fed, the Americans handed out chocolate bars, packaged crackers, coffee, and tinned meat.[7] In Tilly's first shy encounter with the tall, broad-shouldered Americans, she was surprised by their welcoming smiles and grateful for their kind gestures. The food offered by the Americans helped to alleviate her seemingly ever-present hunger and buoy her spirits.

As the days passed on their journey south, Tilly formed a plan. She would continue to accompany the wounded soldier; his presence afforded her protection from thieves wandering the roads. She would seek employment with the American occupying force, rumored to be setting up their Bavarian headquarters in Munich. Her knowledge of the English language, learned in high school, was very good, and she thought they would need translators. With this plan in mind, her mood brightened, and she began to enjoy the exploration of new sights on her journey. Tilly's ability to embrace the future with positive expectations became a characteristic that carried her through worrisome situations in her life.

Fifty-eight kilometers south of Hof, they entered the town of Bayreuth, founded in the eleventh century. With its narrow cobblestone alleyways and long market square flanked by Gothic, Baroque, and Rococo buildings, the town was a medieval showcase despite the destruction of a third of its structures by bombing. From Bayreuth, there were two possible routes to Munich: through the former regional Nazi military headquarters of Nuremberg or via the ancient Roman outpost of Regensburg. In sharing news of conditions found on the road with passing refugees, Tilly learned that most of Nuremberg had been destroyed by heavy bombs and fierce street battles, so they decided to veer east from Bayreuth to connect with the road to Regensburg.

After walking another 60 km, they came to Weiden in der Oberplatz, an old settlement that had straddled a major trade route between the Germanic Empire and Bohemia in the Middle Ages. Entering the western end of the city, they cautiously picked their way around a deserted Wehrmacht barracks to enter the city square, once a complex of Nazi military and administrative offices but now a burned heap of rubble. On April 5, 1945, Allied bombers had dropped 51 explosive and over 1,000 firebombs to level Weiden's Nazi presence.[8] Instead of finding a secure place to rest, they were disheartened to see a heavily bombed wreckage overrun with an influx of refugees, all seeking shelter and food, like themselves. The visible tension created by overcrowding and suffering was almost unbearable, and she wanted to leave.

Just outside of town, they stumbled across Stalag XIIIB, a prisoner-of-war camp that the Americans had liberated on April 22, 1945.[9] Shacks that had confined thousands of prisoners from a multitude of nations now housed refugees. The grim reality of a Nazi prisoner-of-war camp shocked Tilly. Only in recent days had she begun to hear whispers of appalling conditions found at liberated camps, stories of starvation, disease, and torture, and wondered how they could have existed. During the war, she was unaware of what occurred inside the camps. She was haunted by the truth that had been revealed to her. Should she have known? Was her ignorance because of lies spread by Third Reich tyrants or an uneasiness that was best not examined too closely? As a German, would she be condemned for Nazi brutality? These questions, with no ready answers, left her despondent.

She was just so tired. It was the end of summer, and she had traveled 230 km since leaving Thalheim. Buying what little food they could find on the black market, Tilly and her companion wearily trudged 80 more kilometers to Regensburg, a regal city on the banks of the Danube River. Originally a Celtic settlement dating to 500 BC, the site became a Roman bastion guarding the Roman Empire's northern frontier from Germanic hordes. Medieval citizens built their city around and on top of the remains of Roman stone blocks, proudly affirming Regensburg's long history. Into this culturally rich city the Nazis thrust a Messerschmitt Bf 109 aircraft factory and an oil refinery connected to a sizable rail system. The Allies bombed it with gusto. Thankfully, the rest of the city was mostly left intact. Regensburg surrendered to the 71st Division of the U.S. Army without a fight on April 27, 1945,[10] and reconstruction of bombed sections was already underway. Tilly found the city overflowing with Ukrainian refugees, displaced Germans from Eastern Europe, and bombed-out urban dwellers. Hunger, fear, and the search for family and home were all driving forces behind Regensburg's growing population. Lacking the relief she desperately sought, Tilly turned away from Regensburg toward the road leading south.

As they neared the town of Freising, 40 km outside of Munich, Tilly's companion bid her *Auf Wiedersehen*. He eagerly looked forward to reuniting with his parents. The turmoil of events had brought these young people together by chance, and while they had benefited from fellowship, they were ready to forget the past and the wretched memories of what they had seen on the road. They each sought a fresh start with no reminders. Tilly scanned the flat Bavarian plain and the two small hills before her and alone walked into the town of Freising in August, determined to find a way to live in postwar Germany. She had traveled nearly 400 km since leaving Thalheim and, at age nineteen, yearned to be happy again.

# PART II
# Conquered Haven

## Chapter 3. Finding Relief in Freising

The twin towers of Saint Mary and Saint Corbinian Cathedral shone white and stately against the afternoon sky, inviting Tilly into Freising like welcoming beacons of reassurance. What began as a simple monastery established in 720 by Saint Corbinian evolved into the ecclesiastical center of the Duchy of Bavaria complete with a Romanesque Cathedral of the Blessed Virgin on one hill, and the Weihenstephan Benedictine monastery on the second hill. For over a thousand years, the prince-bishops, clerics, and monastics residing on the two hills shaped the cultural, intellectual, and religious affairs of the inhabitants of Freising, the oldest city on the Isar River.[1]

Walking through Freising, Tilly saw that Nazi symbols and names had been removed from buildings and thoroughfares since the city's surrender to American forces on April 29. The purge of any visible Nazi signs from German society was one of the first acts demanded by the American military commander, Captain Albert G. Snow.[2] Tilly was relieved to see the city recovering from an Allied air raid and artillery shelling that had damaged the railway station, factories, and nearly 200 buildings.[3]

**Freising with the Isar River and cathedral towers at the top (white circle); St. George's Church, located at the Marienplatz (white star), is in the foreground, circa 1946.**[4]

At a prewar population of about 19,800, the city was straining to accommodate more than 27,700 people when she arrived, while the outlying district prewar population of 34,700 had jumped by 50 percent.[5] The influx of homeless and desperate people into Freising and the outlying district posed a serious issue. Unknowingly, Tilly had become part of a problem for the Americans—controlling and sheltering dislocated civilians walking into town. As defined by the U.S. Army, a dislocated civilian is either a refugee fleeing their country, an internally displaced person fleeing their home, or an evacuee forcibly removed by authorities. All three types of dislocated civilians were trickling into Freising, but soon liberated foreign workers and concentration camp survivors would complicate the problem. Estimates suggested that seven million people were on the move in Western Europe during the summer of 1945.⁶

**Freising's *Rathaus*. St. George's Church bell tower is right; St. Mary's statue sits in the middle of the Marienplatz, 1946.**

Tilly arrived in the town's beautiful Marienplatz, a large stone-cobbled public square set in the old quarter featuring a statue dedicated to Saint Mary erected in the 1600s. The square was flanked by the Gothic church of St. George and the *Rathaus,* with its large clock embedded in a muraled facade. She didn't know what to expect as she entered the *Rathaus*. Would she find disorganized city administrators confused about conducting business under military occupation? Her worries eased when she found clerks tending to the people's requests in an orderly manner. She asked a clerk what jobs were available—the same question she had repeated at towns on her journey through the American zone. Fortunately, the U.S. Army was holding opening ceremonies for the Weihenstephan Agricultural and Technical School for American soldiers on the day she arrived in Fresing, August 12, 1945. She learned that the school needed secretarial help.

A month earlier, the 115th Cavalry Group of the 20th Corps had discovered the Weihenstephan school while securing the perimeter around Freising and found its facilities untouched by Allied air attacks. The army quickly incorporated the school into educational programs, conceived by Generals George C. Marshall and Dwight D. Eisenhower to prepare soldiers slated for discharge from the European theatre for a job in civilian life. The programs assisted soldiers in learning vocations, achieving a high school diploma, or advancing their college studies. By October 1945, nearly three hundred schools were operating throughout the American zone, offering more than one hundred courses.[7]

The schools kept soldiers occupied while they awaited transport home.[8] On VE Day, there were 1,622,000 American soldiers in Germany. When the shooting ended, only a fraction was needed as an occupying force, with the rest scheduled for either redeployment to the Pacific theater or discharge. The War Department anticipated demobilizing 600,000 soldiers, and everyone wanted to go home faster than the army could move them. With ships and planes dedicated to the war in the Pacific, transport means were limited. It became clear that hundreds of thousands of men would have to wait months before their turn came to be shipped home. Impatient men could have become a monumental morale problem. The schools served a vital function in diverting frustration into education.⁹

Excited to hear about positions available to German women at the Weihenstephan school, Tilly asked how she could apply. Quietly determined to pursue her ambitions, Tilly approached life with an uncommon grit. While she understood it might be unrealistic to expect too much, she was nonetheless optimistic about finding a job with the Americans.

The official at the *Rathaus* gave her directions to the school offices in the sprawling Schlüterhof estate requisitioned by the U.S. Army, located about a kilometer outside the city center. At the Schlüterhof, she was interviewed by First Lieutenant Army Air Corps Eugene R. Schleiger, a native of Nebraska. As an instructor in the Physics Department holding a master's degree in physics, Schleiger was pleased with Tilly's appearance, knowledge of science, experience at AEG, and fluency in English. At 5 feet and 4 inches, with light brown eyes, reddish-brown hair, and a ready smile, Tilly radiated charm, energy, and intelligence. Schleiger decided to send her to be screened by the Counter Intelligence Corps (CIC) to determine if she was eligible for employment.

On May 1, just two days after what the locals called "the American invasion," the CIC had set up shop in room 24 of the *Rathaus* to investigate the populace for membership in the Nazi Party.¹⁰ Understandably, people were nervous about what the CIC would uncover. Tilly joined the long line of citizens summoned to the CIC office awaiting questioning and was eventually referred to a Special Branch Officer assigned to the Freising Detachment. Special Branch personnel were in charge of denazification, a mandate to purge German society of Nazi ideology. A big part of this strategy was to bar Nazi

Party members from jobs with the U.S. Army or in German public and private sectors, as determined through an extensive background check including a lengthy questionnaire called a *Fragebogen*.[11]

The Special Branch officer warned Tilly that lying carried criminal penalties and to answer questions honestly about her private life, past employment, and membership in organizations. Because the Nazis compelled every young German to join Hitler Youth and the National Labor Service, barring civilians from these organizations would have eliminated nearly the entire population from employment; consequently, Special Branch just sought Nazi Party members. When she submitted her completed *Fragebogen,* the officer told her the review process would take several weeks. The process involved counterintelligence agents who checked names against Nazi Party rolls and police records and conducted interviews with past employers whenever possible.[12] She heard of several Nazi Party members who had been flushed out, arrested, and placed temporarily in the old seventeenth-century Fischergasse prison before being transported to the Dachau concentration camp—now holding Nazis instead of Jews.[13] Other than these instances, most residents returned home feeling relieved after their CIC interrogations.

While waiting to hear about her employment eligibility status, the housing authority assigned Tilly to an empty bed in a kindergarten that was being used to shelter the unhoused. Dislocated civilians were sent to shelters in converted gymnasiums, abandoned hotels, vacant dormitories, and dormant kindergartens until the housing authority could find them rooms in the Freising district, which were in short supply. Some refugees remained in these temporary shelters for several years.[14] Housing had been severely reduced due to damage by air raids and requisitioning by the occupying forces. The housing situation had reached such a critical point that it verged on catastrophe. The ongoing requisition of numerous homes to quarter troops and their arriving dependents turned the Bavarians' initial relief at the Americans ending the terrible war into deep resentment toward the invaders who were taking their houses. As their responsibilities increased, the number of military government personnel in Bavaria rose from one hundred in May to nearly five hundred by the fall of 1945.[15]

The room she shared with other women at the shelter was small and crowded but well-lit from a bank of windows along a wall. The U.S. Army supplied blankets to the refugees. The shelters bustled with newcomers settling in while leaders directed repairs and winterization projects. Winter was approaching, and there was a critical coal shortage for civilian domestic heating. Bavarian coal mines were operating, but the occupation forces required such large quantities—as much as 80 percent of production—that the coal remaining was insufficient to meet the demands for restarting rail transportation and industry, heating homes, and cooking.[16] Consequently, it was necessary to repair broken windows and install handmade woodstoves in the shelter buildings as precautions against the cold. City officials announced that people should collect firewood from the nearby forest to obtain the fuel needed for winter.

> Firewood felling for the winter of 1945–46: the male population of the city and district of Freising is

requested to make themselves available to produce the necessary fuel. The requested amount of firewood for the community can only be provided with the involvement of all. Payment for the work is a decent wage if the work is fairly brisk. Since a coal allocation for the winter is not expected, in the interest of the people of Freising, firewood production is crucial.[17]

Volunteers marched into the forest and, under the supervision of forestry officials, used hatchets and handsaws to fell trees, saw and split logs, and carry them back to the shelters. In the evenings, as fires were lit, the thick smell of green wood smoke filled the air, clung to Tilly's clothes, and made her cough.

One incident at the shelter deeply humiliated her. Like all dislocated civilians entering refugee camps, army personnel dusted her with DDT powder to prevent the spread of deadly louse-borne typhus. Knowing that typhus had caused massive deaths among soldiers on the Eastern Front during World War I, the Allies wanted to avoid a repeat of that horror.[18] Although the dusting only lasted a few seconds, she felt embarrassed as the insecticide was power-hosed up her skirt, down her waistband, and inside her blouse. For good measure, the relief worker doused her hair with gasoline to kill any lice. It burned her scalp and smelled awful! It took many shampoo sessions to rid her hair of gasoline fumes. After arriving, refugees endured repeated treatments of DDT dusting in the following months, so Tilly hoped to find alternative housing before the next dusting treatment was scheduled.

To escape the confines of the shelter, Tilly spent her days exploring the area, but she was careful to avoid the curfew times established by the military government. Civilians were prohibited from being on the streets between 9:30 p.m. and 5 a.m. The punishment for being caught during the curfew was a fine of up to 100 Reichsmarks or ten days imprisonment. A high-pitched siren signaled a 30-second warning to people who were slow to move. She always had to carry her military government-issued registration card in case of sudden checks. Soldiers would take anyone without identification to spend several hours in the old Fischergasse prison.[19]

Walking on the city's south side, she found people attempting to reestablish their everyday lives, relaxing on the banks of the Isar River, laughing and enjoying being together. She often walked on paths along the Isar River which wound through the city. She found shady trees to sit under while contemplating what she had been through and what her future might hold.

A path along the Isar River.[20]

She was relieved that the bombing had ended, and the wailing sirens that had chased people into cellars had ceased. She no longer worried about whether she would be alive tomorrow, and while food was meager, she did not fear starvation. The tension she had long held under the specter of death from bombs, bullets, and the Russians was fading. The end of the war meant the beginning of opportunity and freedom because despotism had been swept away. It was easy to shake off the Nazi mentality—what had the Nazis done but drag everyone into unparalleled suffering and despair? The Germanic people had produced acclaimed composers, artists, writers, philosophers, and scientists for a thousand years, contributing significantly to Western Civilization. Why should they be defined by twelve years under a madman's rule? She realized that growing up in Hitler's repressive Third Reich had allowed her no room for self-determination. Sitting by the Isar River, she felt an emerging sense of freedom and hope replacing the war-weary uncertainty she had carried for so long. As she watched industrious repair crews steadily erase the evidence of destruction and reestablish order, she saw resilient and hardy German people rebuilding and dreaming of possibilities and she smiled.

*** 

Thorough screening for Nazi Party members by the military's denazification officers was a huge and time-consuming task that they would eventually pass on to the Germans themselves. In the meantime, Tilly had to wait while tens of thousands of Germans in Freising were evaluated. During the waiting period, Tilly celebrated her twentieth birthday alone, but she was thankful to be healthy and in a safe place. Finally, she received a recommendation for employment from the Special Branch office. This document gave the green light to Schleiger to hire her as the Physics Department secretary. She was thrilled! For the Americans to take a chance on her and provide her an opportunity for a fresh start meant two things to her: that she had value in the eyes of an American army officer and that, as a German, she had a chance at reconciliation with the Americans for the wrongs committed by her people during the war.

She was hired near the end of the term so she would have to wait to begin work until the next term started on January 7, 1946. To prepare her for her first day on the job, Schleiger gave Tilly an overview of the school and its operation. A Bavarian university focused on the agricultural, horticultural, and brewing sciences had existed since the 1800s on the grounds of the former Weihenstephan Benedictine monastery, where monks had established the long tradition of brewing. The U.S. Army took advantage of the equipment in the university's classrooms and experimental greenhouses left behind and adapted course offerings for soldiers in the 20th Corps. American educators within the army were assigned to teach the courses. Soldiers returning to their farms could take agrarian courses such as dairy and creamery operations, fruit and vegetable cultivation, poultry, pork, and beef production, crop management, and soil conservation. In addition, traditional high school and junior college level courses such as biology, chemistry, calculus, and physics were offered.

The four hundred soldiers accepted for each eight-week term were housed on the second floor of the three-story Schlüterhof, located about 200 meters down the hill from the school.[21] The Schlüterhof was a large estate consisting of an agricultural test center, dairy operation, and family residence built in 1912 by Anton Schlüter, the owner of a multi-fuel engine factory and iron foundry.[22] In the center of the second floor were offices for the school instructors, a recreational hall for students, and bathrooms.[23]

**The Schlüterhof, 1946.**

**School headquarters at the Schlüterhof, 1946.**

In a stroke of good fortune, a city housing administrator informed Tilly that a room was available for her to rent in a private home on Fürstendamm. Tilly was immensely grateful to have a bed in a home after spending many nights in refugee camps since leaving Thalheim. Although she was alone and had no word from her family, Tilly's Christmas in 1945 was not entirely barren. The winter weather was unusually warm, and the U.S. Army's food office released extra rations of sugar and flour.[24] With less cold and hunger, her mood brightened.

*\*\*\**

At the start of the school term, Tilly walked into her office with a sense of purpose, feeling she was part of something important. Her secretarial duties included the usual office work, such as typing, mimeographing, and filing. But as Schleiger became aware of Tilly's knowledge and interest in the coursework, he gave her additional responsibilities, such as grading student examination papers, maintaining the physics equipment storage room, and translating chemistry and physics passages from English to German and vice versa. He later commented, "Tilly has a good knowledge of English, both written and oral, and her familiarity with scientific terms has been especially valuable to this department. Her general ability, diligence, and willingness to learn have been excellent." Tilly found pleasure in performing her job well. She regained a sense of dignity that she had lost during the chaotic weeks following the fall of the Third Reich.

Tilly recaptured her youthful days spent with girlfriends in the RAD when she met other *Mädels* working as cleaning women or office help at the school. The young women—Kläre, Lilo, Maria, Gertrud, Rosi, Martha, and Tilly—quickly formed close bonds borne from shared experiences of adversity, loneliness, and anxiety that their security could be suddenly snatched away. As an outsider, Tilly had struggled to find acceptance in the conservative, inward-looking Bavarian culture of Freising, where locals treated dislocated civilians as second-class.[25] She had felt resentful stares from residents for taking up scarce resources and working for the invaders.

While diverse in their backgrounds, the school was a common factor that fostered camaraderie among the young women. They were delighted to acquire a scarce bolt of checkered fabric, which they made into hand-sewn dresses. Their matching outfits further strengthened their bond of friendship.

She noticed soldiers at the school had more advanced cameras than her old Agfa box, such as the Kodak 35 Rangefinder. This camera offered faster shutter speeds and manual focus for sharper prints, a film with more exposures per roll, and a synchronized flash. When she discovered that the school had a photography lab stocked with supplies at her disposal, she saved her salary to buy a Kodak camera from one of the soldiers.

Inspired by owning a camera again, she resumed taking photos and occasionally received tips from men enrolled in photography courses at the school. Her photos reflected the close circle of people who supported her and the experiences that influenced her thoughts and emotions. The soldiers enjoyed practicing their photography skills by taking pictures of the young women. These lighthearted sessions were enjoyable for everyone involved.

Tilly's daily interactions with the soldiers were friendly, resulting in a collegial feeling toward the American military that she held for the rest of her life. In turn, the soldiers enjoyed exchanging good-natured banter with the women. The friendships that developed between the women and the soldiers, shaped by their everyday experiences at the school, fostered a mutual trust and understanding.

German staff of the Schlüterhof. From left Lilo, Tilly, Maria, Kläre, Martha, and Gertrud, 1946.[26]

German staff of the Schlüterhof pose for soldiers practicing photography, 1946.[27]

Also working at the school was a German woman named Gertrud Schumacher. Although Gertrud was older than Tilly, the two became friends. As a beautiful and intelligent brunette, Gertrud caught Schleiger's attention. Gertrud valued the admiration of a confident and good-natured American officer and, in time, began affectionately calling Schleiger by his middle name, Rex.

**First Lieutenant Eugene R. Schleiger (left) and Gertrud Schumacher (right), 1946.**

Initially, Gertrud and Rex kept their budding courtship discreet because early military policy from Washington discouraged fraternization between soldiers and enemy civilians. The U.S. Army Handbook G-3 called for "the avoidance of mingling with Germans upon terms of friendliness, familiarity, or intimacy, whether individually or in groups, in official or unofficial dealings."[28] Memos were issued to newly installed military government commanders on how the troops were to conduct themselves. "Without demonstrating vengefulness or spite, the behavior of the Americans should express cool hostility and distaste . . . It should be made clear to the Germans that they are responsible for the Second World War and will not be forgiven for their terrible oppression of other peoples under German rule."[29] Handshakes were forbidden, and, of course, sexual relationships.

However, Washington's ideas of meting out retribution did not resonate well with the soldiers on the ground who witnessed sick, hungry, and frightened people reeling from destruction and desperate for peace. They needed help, especially the children. Nearly 80 percent of soldiers interviewed said they had a favorable impression of the German people, and less than half blamed them for the war. No official memo was going to stop a kind soldier from giving out candy to children or prevent a lonely American man from socializing with a German woman. The military's nonfraternization policy was impractical and was given a fleeting glance by the soldiers before being completely ignored. Eventually, the army viewed nonfraternization as a roadblock to Germany's cultural rehabilitation, and Eisenhower ended the policy.[30]

As U.S. military policy toward enemy civilians relaxed, Rex's apprehension about his intimate relationship with Gertrud eased. He decided to take Gertrud with him for a weekend trip to the alpine Bavarian town of Garmisch[31], located 128 km south of Freising. They planned to ski and sightsee with friends. The American zone offered a variety of scenic attractions for soldiers on recreational leave, especially in Bavaria. A standard joke among the U.S. military was that the Russians received Germany's agriculture, the British acquired the industry, and the Americans got the scenery.[32]

On an early spring day in 1946, Tilly was invited to accompany Gertrud, Rex, and several officers and German women who worked at the school to Garmisch. Tilly had heard about Garmisch when she had lived in Berlin. Before the war, many Berliners journeyed to the Alps for winter vacation. As the group traveled by train through the dark green forest of the valley, she was excited to see the highest peak in the Bavarian Alps, the Zugspitze, emerge from the fir trees.

**Zugspitze railway station in Garmisch.**

**Children follow the soldiers as Tilly smiles.**[33]

**Frescoes displayed on Garmisch houses.**

As the group walked from the train station into town, a crowd of small children appeared and surrounded the soldiers, hoping for gifts of gum and chocolate. American soldiers commonly attracted children. Walking through Garmisch, the group admired rows of small shops offering hand-worked silver jewelry, amber beads, intricate wood carvings, and Bavarian costumes. Gabled houses of brightly colored plaster and timber were adorned with religious frescoes.

The Zugspitze.

A gondola takes people up the mountain.

From left: Mr. Teschler, Gertrud, and Rex at Garmisch, 1946.

Crowding into a gondola, the group glided up the mountain, where there were large areas of snow for the skiers, interspersed with sunlit patches of dry moss and rock for the sunbathers. Behind the camera, Tilly captured the happiness of her friends, while in front of the lens, she was caught gaily sunbathing with her pals. With lifted spirits, the *Mädels* put the terrible war behind them with laughter, and celebrated life.

**Tilly (middle) and friends sunbathing at Garmisch, April 1946.**[34]

On March 1, 1946, as part of a planned demobilization of combat troops, army leadership inactivated the 20th Corps, transported the soldiers stateside, and pivoted toward postwar military security and governance in Germany. With only a few students left to take courses, the army ordered the Weihenstephan Agricultural and Technical School to close on April 12. Tilly was heartbroken at the sudden news. She had only been at her job in the Physics Department for a few months and it seemed too soon to lose her job and her new friendships. Tilly's struggle to find stability mirrored the experiences of millions of Germans in early 1946. What was she going to do now?

## Chapter 4. Embracing a Democratic Life

Schleiger received orders to close the Physics Department with mixed feelings. While eager to return to Kansas and advance his teaching career, he was reluctant to leave Gertrud behind. Tilly was sorry to see her boss unsettled and helped him to complete tasks in the brief time remaining. They had to reassign or dispose of classroom and office supplies and equipment, arrange transportation to the port of Bremerhaven where the instructors would board a freighter bound for New York, and assemble the necessary paperwork so Gertrud could apply for non-quota immigration as Schleiger's fiancée under the War Brides Act of 1945. Schleiger took the time to write a letter of recommendation for Tilly and contacted the military commander for *Stadtkreis-Landkreis* (city-district) Freising Detachment, encouraging him to consider her for a position as an office clerk and interpreter.

Captain Kenneth S. Cochrane, Freising Detachment G-231 Special Branch, Company E, 3rd Military Government Regiment, received Schleiger's letter of recommendation for Tilly and replied, "Okay, I'll give her a try." Cochrane, a native of New York, had enlisted in the army in 1940 and, by April 1946, was an experienced and war-weary soldier, aged beyond his thirty-eight years from the demands of his responsibilities.

Assured of another job with the U.S. Army, Tilly was relieved to have forestalled the prospect of poverty, a hardship that would haunt her repeatedly throughout her life. Working for the Americans, she would earn a paycheck and be able to afford renting a room. She was thankful to avoid the refugee camps, where the city's newly assembled healthcare ministry had reported hundreds of active cases of tuberculosis.[1]

Tilly began her job as an office clerk and interpreter for Cochrane on April 15, 1946, three days after saying goodbye to her friends in the Physics Department. The walk from her room on Fürstendamm to the military government offices at the *Rathaus* was just a third of a kilometer. The route took her through Freising's historic quarter along Obere Hauptstraße, where ornamented facades on buildings painted in cheerful colors cast a fairy-tale illusion over a somber reality.

**Ornamented facades adorn buildings of the Obere Hauptstraße.**

On Tilly's first day at her new job, Cochrane summarized the history of the occupation for her, which had entered its second year. Leaning back in his office chair, a contrail of smoke drifted through the air from his ever-present cigarette as he began to share the dry facts. At end of the war, the U.S. military had assumed responsibility for the health and welfare of millions of stunned and distraught Germans in the American zone, which swelled in population from a massive influx of dislocated civilians. The scarcity of housing was the result of the Allied bombing campaign, which had dropped 370,000 tons of bombs on Germany, creating unprecedented piles of rubble.[2] Additional problems included the imminent risk of mass starvation, threats of epidemics, and the fear that latent Naziism would reassert itself. While the last thing the army wanted to do was preside over the occupation of a destroyed country, they saw it as imperative to denazify the German culture and reform German society with American democratic ideals before returning the governance of Germany to the Germans.[3] President Harry S. Truman agreed with army commanders to shift control of Germany to civilian hands as soon as practical because "the military should not have governmental responsibilities beyond the requirements of military operations."[4]

OMGUS, the army's organization charged with governing the American occupation zone in Germany, had been established by General Lucius D. Clay to administer civil affairs during the occupation. As Military Governor, Clay governed the American zone from his headquarters in Berlin from January 1, 1946, through 1949.[5] He faced a herculean job of reassembling a broken postwar society.

45

**U.S. occupied zone of Germany, excluding the Berlin sector and Bremen enclave.**

OMGUS was composed of five military government offices or Lands: a Berlin sector in the Soviet zone, a Bremen enclave in the British zone, Greater Hessen, Baden-Württemberg, and Bavaria—the largest Land, and unique from the rest in being predominately Catholic. The area of the American zone, not including the Berlin quarter and Bremen enclave, was 106,190 square kilometers, with an estimated population of fifteen and a half million in the fall of 1945.[6] Each Land was divided into several districts, known as *Regierungsbezirke*, which consisted of a central headquarters and numerous field detachments deployed in selected towns.

Field detachments, which performed occupation duties at the local level, typically consisted of three to four officers and five to six enlisted men. Special Branches worked with detachments to tackle specialized duties in support of the military government.[7] Detachment commanders faced a daunting array of challenges well outside of the soldier's traditional combat role. Nonetheless, they pulled out Army Field Manual 27-5 and set to work directing actions in:

- Public health (reestablish local health agencies to care for the sick and wounded, contain communicable diseases with sanitation, vaccination, and DDT dusting, repair water and sewage lines).
- Public welfare (set up local agencies to help the army locate supplies and distribute food and clothing).
- Resources (salvage collection, procure and provide materials for rebuilding, create a labor exchange).
- Utilities and communication (repair electric, gas, and telephone lines, restore postal and radio services).
- Commerce (set up a pricing and rationing system, suppress black markets).
- Legal (establish and publish regulations, organize courts, bring war criminals to justice).
- Fiscal (commence local tax collection, assure proper custody of abandoned property).[8]

According to Army Field Manual 27-5, commanders should be firm but fair and without vengeance in dealing with the defeated Germans, keeping in mind the goal of rebuilding a self-governing Germany purged of Nazis and politically reformed along democratic lines.[9] One of the first steps the detachment commanders took toward their aim of relinquishing control of government functions to the locals was denazification—the removal of former Nazi Party officials from positions of power. Denazification was essential to the establishment of free, democratic elections.[10] Cochrane's work in Freising Detachment G-231, Special Branch, concerned the denazification and democratization of the inhabitants of Freising.

Tilly became instantly immersed in the overwhelming mission of OMGUS. As an office clerk, she watched the soldiers fulfill their occupation responsibilities. It pleased her to see the Freising Detachment officers learn from the German people, adapting policy to the circumstances. These instances of empathy expressed by the soldiers solidified her favorable view of Americans and their democratic principles.

As Tilly carried out her duties, she witnessed the struggle between the Americans and Germans regarding the scope and intent of denazification. The military government's proclamation of Law Number 8, which mandated sweeping denazification measures, was judged by the Germans as draconian and caused them great despair. In many instances, it removed the very people from office that were needed to run industries and local governments effectively. Often, the most competent German officials had belonged to the Nazi Party, although many argued that membership was a mandate for conducting business in the Third Reich and not a declaration of their ideology.[11] The shortage of experienced non-Nazis in administrative positions left Cochrane and his peers wondering if stringent adherence to Law Number 8 might jeopardize the military government's effectiveness.

Tilly watched Cochrane wrestle between his duty to follow the army denazification policy and his desire to restart local government and economic activity as soon as possible. Cochrane was cynical about the efficacy of denazification anyway, so it was not difficult for him to prioritize war recovery over a thorough denazification of Freising society.[12] Tilly thought this was a realistic approach because the influx of former Nazi followers into official positions was unavoidable. The individuals who were influential during the Nazi regime were still influential—they were prominent businessmen, manufacturers, and landowners who continued to exert influence and skew political priorities through their money and personal connections.

The measures taken by Special Branch to diminish Nazi influence in German society, including the elimination of Nazi symbols, the removal of militaristic Nazi Party members from positions of authority, and the swift prosecution of Nazi war criminals, would have to suffice. By June 1946, OMGUS extricated itself from a deeply unpopular process by transferring the responsibility for denazification to city investigative tribunals, the *Kreisspruchkammern*.[13]

While denazification occurred early in the occupation, democratization came later. In late 1945 and early 1946, most Germans had little interest in participating in political activities related to democracy—their attention was focused on the daily quest to improve their financial and food situations. With starvation looming, democracy had little value. As long as economic hardship continued, the emergence of democracy in postwar Germany would be hindered by disenchantment, distrust, and resentment of the occupying powers. Surprisingly, the notion of American democracy gradually seeped into German society from descriptions of how Americans lived in German-language magazines, newspapers, radio programs, and films.[14]

Tilly embraced this new vision of a democratic life. She watched films shown by the military government in Freising, but discovered that a richer education venue was in Munich—the Amerikahaus. This information center, established by the Munich military government, housed a movie theater, classroom, exhibition hall, library, and reading room.[15] The idea behind the information center was to foster an understanding of American culture and politics. On her occasional days off over the next three years, she took a 40 km bus ride from Freising to Munich to spend time in the Amerikahaus, where she watched Hollywood movies and documentaries. She often attended lectures by detachment officers about such topics as "The Jury System" or "The Press." She liked to wander through exhibitions about great American figures like George Washington and Abraham Lincoln. In the library, she found books about democratic principles that were printed in German, obtained by OMGUS from German communities in the U.S. Tilly always mingled with a crowd of people at the Amerikahaus, which was a major entertainment attraction, drawing an average of 80,000 visitors a month from surrounding towns.[16] The center provided Bavarians with welcome distractions from their daily struggles and a warm place to spend a winter day when coal was difficult to come by.[17]

While exploring Munich with her camera, the thirteenth-century domed towers of the Frauenkirche captivated her. She wound her way through rubble ringing lots stripped naked of their buildings by bombs, and passed by medieval stone walls scarred by bullet tracings, before reaching the city's cathedral. Though the city had suffered severe war damage, it was bustling with movement—cars and cyclists wove through scores of people striding purposefully toward the restoration of normal lives. Secure with a full belly, safe housing, and a job with the U.S. Army, Tilly's focus shifted from her immediate priorities to an examination of events influencing others, and her photos began to reflect this change.

**Munich, 1948.**

**Towers of the Frauenkirche behind strafed walls, 1948.**

**Munich's *Rathaus*, 1948.**

In spring 1946, Tilly watched the military government prepare for the first *Stadtkreis* and *Landkreis* elections in Bavaria since 1933. Freising Detachment staff worked overtime to organize the elections. The staff made a big effort to achieve Clay's policy of "throwing more responsibility on the Germans and lessening the American taxpayer's burden" by facilitating a rapid return to local political control.[18] The staff supported the establishment of anti-Nazi political parties and in December, political parties such as the Christian Social Union, Social Democrats, and Communist parties began to assemble. The staff registered voters, informed them of their rights, and encouraged participation in the upcoming elections.[19]

On April 28, 1946, the first election for the Freising *Landkreis* council took place. Tilly wasn't surprised that the party aligned with Catholic social philosophy, the conservative Christian Social Union, scored the most seats, followed by Social Democrat party members. These two parties then selected their administrator, the *Landrat*. On May 26, 1946, the Christian Social Union party emerged as the winner of the city elections, and the city council elected their lord mayor, the *Oberbürgermeister*.

In conversations overheard while shopping, Tilly discovered that some Freising residents were suspicious about the recent election results. They didn't believe the elected local officials were independent but instead acted as puppets of the U.S. Army.[20] Tilly knew that these beliefs had some truth. The military government expected local officials to cooperate with their policies, potentially contradicting the will of the people. However, until the Germans achieved the societal changes necessary for an enduring democracy, the military government would maintain its oversight of political activity.

Reflecting on her communications with Cochrane in the office, Tilly thought about the changes sought by the military government. A high priority in 1946 was addressing the inequality present in Freising society. Had Freising integrated dislocated civilians into their community? No, not yet. Residents treated dislocated people like Tilly as if they were inferior. Freising officials dismissed the notion of assimilating refugees because they didn't think the present conditions were permanent.[21] Their negligent attitude just prolonged the problem of marginalized people living on the edges of society and barred them from civic engagement.

Worse were the lingering aspects of antisemitism. Carefully nourished and fostered during twelve years of intensive Nazi propaganda, antisemitic attitudes were not quickly discarded. The spirit of Nazism continued to linger in schools, where some Jewish children reported feeling threatened.[22] Tilly overheard familiar complaints, such as, "Most Jews are engaged in black market activities, cheating the hard-working population!" or, "Jews are parasites on the German economy and should either start working or leave the country."[23]

Had the war and occupation changed the character of the people to the extent that they were less susceptible to the influence of demagogues playing on nationalist and racist sentiments? Maybe, a little, but Tilly didn't expect to see widespread changes in attitudes anytime soon. She suspected that distorted perceptions and long-held prejudices would likely prolong the efforts to achieve societal equality in communities throughout Germany. As an outsider in Freising, she empathized with others in similar situations—displaced from home, feeling excluded, yet longing to belong. Wanting to offer support she wished she had received, she vowed to respect those whose cultures and identities differed from her own. She mused, "After all, aren't equity and inclusion core principles of a democracy?"

\*\*\*

Although a local government was in place to shoulder more responsibility for public welfare, soldiers in the Freising Detachment had no time to catch their breath. A food crisis was approaching, not only in the western occupation zones, but across much of Europe as well. Farmland to the east had been lost to the Soviet Union due to zonal partition—land that had accounted for 35 percent of Germany's prewar food production. With less land to farm, few people to farm it, and reduced quantities of seeds, fertilizer, and livestock, food became a critical factor in the stability of postwar western Germany. Food production and distribution in the American occupation zone were assisted in every way possible by the U.S. Army, which supplied fuel, seeds, and fertilizer, set up storage and transportation infrastructure, reopened farm machinery repair shops, and restarted processing plants. Despite these herculean efforts, hunger remained a harsh reality for many people, especially in the cities.[24]

To distribute food to people in the American occupation zone, the military government continued the rationing system set up by the Nazis. Those civilians not involved in heavy work were allowed a maximum of 1,550 calories per day, allocated through ration cards. Tilly knew that, in reality, the average person in Freising only received around 1,000 calories per day. The local civilian government was responsible for ensuring that district farmers met their crop quotas, but food supplies fell short. A typical week's ration consisted of 3 pounds of bread, 4 ounces of meat, 2 ounces of butter, 7 ounces of sugar, 5 ounces of macaroni, and 6 pounds of potatoes, with a few ounces of vegetables, if available. Only children up to age six were allowed a quart of milk a week.[25]

**The children of Freising suffered from scarce food supplies in 1946.**

As an employee of the military government, Tilly received daytime meals as part of her pay and thus fared better than those who relied on just their government-issued rations. Those with inadequate rations turned to the black market. Or they went to the country to barter whatever goods they still possessed with farmers who hoarded their meat and vegetables.[26] To survive, people had no other recourse. The military government attempted to shut down the black market, but since these vendors were everywhere, the black market was "difficult to control."[27]

Tilly was alarmed to see rising community tension as new refugees poured into the district. Residents regarded the refugees as threats, believing that the capacity of the *Landkreis* to absorb more people was nearly exhausted. Tilly suspected that their resentment stemmed from the fear that the needs of the refugees would deplete their already limited food, housing, and material supplies. Tilly's employers shared her worries about the situation. A detachment commander sent a warning to the director of the Intelligence Division, Office of Military Government for Bavaria in Munich, highlighting the dire circumstances he had witnessed.

> The people are becoming weary of the poor economic conditions, food and housing shortages, and restrictions imposed by military government. People tend to find a scapegoat to blame for their difficulties—during the Nazi regime it was the Jews, now it is the dislocated civilians and refugees. People who are experiencing difficulties are attracted to the emotional appeal of a talented demagogue. Underlying prejudices, racism, and nationalism can be fanned into a fire by capable demagogues.[28]

Since the beginning of the occupation, the U.S. military had imported all their food to avoid depleting the already scarce local food supplies. With the developing food crisis, U.S. policymakers in Washington, D.C., reversed a policy implemented early in the postwar period: prohibiting the import of food for the German population. Initially, the prevailing attitude in Washington, D.C., had been that the Germans got themselves into this mess so they could damn well get themselves out of it. However, it became clear that the population could not remain on the low-calorie food rations without severe malnutrition. Addressing military government personnel about the food situation, Clay wrote:

> It was made clear to the Germans that they were to rely on their own production of resources for their livelihood. But the region within the American zone is deficient and falling short of meeting its food requirements. Under the current low ration scales, consumers are forced into the black market to subsist. It does not look like deficits will be alleviated by the projected harvest, and there will be a grave shortage of foods this winter. We can say that they should have thought of that before they started the war and let them starve or survive as best they may. . . .or, we can aid in every way possible the German food production and distribution program. . . .But recognizing that with the indigenous crop there will still be a substantial deficit in a food, a request has already been made to import a quarter of the estimated years' deficit of grain.[29]

While it was not at all certain that Clay would find the imports to support the announced increase, Cochrane was relieved the U.S. had conceded that food would need to be imported to alleviate starvation.

In a similar reversal of policy, the Allies finally allowed relief organizations to distribute provisions in Germany. They had restricted aid believing that the German standard of living should align with the surrounding European nations struggling to recover from Nazi plunder. However, as millions of expellees poured into the diminished German state from Poland, Hungary, Czechoslovakia, Romania, Yugoslavia, the Baltic states, and areas annexed by the Soviet Union, it became clear that widespread famine was imminent. When the International Red Cross began distributing food and supply packets at German refugee camps, a little more weight was lifted from the shoulders of the military government.[30]

\*\*\*

Army policy shifted frequently, but one edict that remained foremost was to minimize occupation costs. Consequently, the army cut German civilian positions within the Freising Detachment. Cochrane informed Tilly that her job was "terminated due to a reduction in indigenous civilian personnel," effective May 31, 1946. He wrote an evaluation complimenting her work as "very satisfactory." Although Tilly had only worked for the military government for six weeks, she had gained a greater understanding of American customs, values, and approaches to problem-solving, which she believed would help her find another job with the occupation forces.

While Tilly sought stability in Freising's rapidly evolving postwar conditions, Grete was planning to leave Austria with Christel and return to an uncertain situation in Berlin. They had been refugees for nearly a year and a half, and in May 1946, they were eager to return home, especially eight-year-old Christel, who had missed her papa. After packing their small bundle of belongings, they embarked on a journey covering over 600 km. Christel recalled, "Our journey back to Berlin took one month, in cattle wagons and many small distances. Once, we had to sleep in a concentration camp, which was changed into a camp for refugees. Here, they sprayed me with insecticide and poured gasoline on my scalp, which burned! To see my dad again was great. But there was still famine."

Concerned with immediate necessities in late spring 1946, most German people were unaware of the rising tension among American military leaders as they watched the Soviet Union impose increasingly authoritarian political and economic controls in their occupation zone. The Soviets restrained the press, harassed anticommunist political figures, and began a campaign of regime change in countries under their influence, including Poland, Czechoslovakia, and Hungary. The confrontation between the Americans and Soviets over geopolitical influence intensified when negotiations on reparations collapsed, leading Clay to halt the delivery of further German industrial machinery, products, and raw materials to the Soviets.[31]

To support the military government's occupation mission in Bavaria, the U.S. Army Air Corps moved the 604th Tactical Control Squadron to Freising in December 1945, where they had set up a radar site to track and control military aircraft. Figuring that the 604th Tactical Control Squadron would maintain a presence in Freising for the foreseeable future, Tilly resolutely set her sights on finding employment with the 604th.

# PART III
# Shifted Alliances

## Chapter 5. New Friendships

"*Eine Putzfrau!*" Tilly mumbled to herself, shaking her head with relief and melancholy. In June 1946, she received word that her application to work as a cleaning woman at the 604th Tactical Control Squadron had been accepted. She was assigned to clean the bachelor officers' quarters (BOQ) in a requisitioned residence on Ganzenmüllerstraße in Freising. Unlike her previous work with the U.S. military, she had not been hired for her intelligence but for physical labor. In her eyes, the job was little better than that of the *Trümmerfrauen*—women who cleared rubble and scavenged bricks from bombed buildings. For a young woman aspiring to better herself and her situation, a position as housekeeper was a humbling fall from the interesting work she had done as a secretary and interpreter for the military government. Still, the job provided the immediate benefits she craved in the postwar turmoil—housing, food, money, security, and safety. Moreover, she would continue to be in the company of Americans.

Tilly had been eight years old when Hitler came to power in 1933, and the society she grew up in no longer existed. In fact, the Allies were waging an active campaign against such a society ever existing again. It was natural for her to define a new normal. As she entered her twenty-first year, her definition of normal gradually began to align with that of the Americans, even though Tilly understood that the American occupying forces had their flaws—they did not always act as benevolent heroes.

The squadron requisitioned hotels and residences to house personnel until they could establish a base, exacerbating Freising's critical housing shortage. The U.S. Army's requisition of houses was a contentious practice that revealed the hypocrisy between the army's stated democratic principles and its actions. The army's policy to prioritize the care of its troops over the needs of the vanquished people compounded the misery of the population. Residents lived in limbo, fearing forced evictions and uncertain about finding accommodation elsewhere. As American soldiers appeared at their doorways, ordering the inhabitants to get out within a day, residents scrambled to collect and load their clothes and food onto handcarts, leaving behind the furniture with profound feelings of sadness and loss. While residents expressed bitter resentment toward the Americans for taking their homes and possessions, the Hague Convention allowed the requisition of property as long as it was used to meet the needs of the occupying army.[1]

The Americans requisitioned a row of houses on Ganzenmüllerstraße. House number 29, a large four-story structure with attractive canted bay windows on the corners, was selected as the 604th BOQ. A Frau evicted from her home on Ganzenmullerstraße later recounted her suffering. "You cannot say what it means to have to leave your house and find shelter somewhere in the most primitive conditions, crammed into the smallest of spaces. It was terrible."[2]

Ganzenmüllerstraße 29, the BOQ of the 604th.

From left: Lt. Browning, Lt. Bell, and Capt. Busher at the BOQ.

Ganzenmüllerstraße 33.

Tilly's private room.

Tilly's accommodations became unstable. She had to move into a dormitory in the Schlüterhof in the fall, then found lodging at another private home in the spring of 1947, before moving into billets for the squadron's female civilian laborers in a spacious, four-story requisitioned house on Ganzenmüllerstraße. Tilly's move into House 33 on

Ganzenmüllerstraße was noticed and resented by the remaining residents on the street. Estranged from her neighbors, Tilly formed close friendships with other girls who lived in or visited the house, including Gusti, Jonni, Hilda, Berta, Ilse, and Fanni. The house was also home to a caretaker and his wife, *Hausmeister* Richard and Ilse Pirkl. Shielding herself from the glares of Freising residents, Tilly spent her time in the company of her roommates. She sympathized with the evicted residents and attempted to reconcile her guilt about living in a home taken by force by recalling the ancient rules of warfare: to the victor go the spoils. Since she worked for the victors, she convinced herself that it was all right to enjoy her new accommodations. However, for a time, the guilt intruded on her peace of mind.

**German staff of the 604th. From left: Hilda, Gusti, and Berta.**

**From left: Tilly, Fanni, and Jonni at Ganzenmüllerstraße 33.[3]**   **Hausmeister Pirkl and his wife.**

The house was well furnished inside, with pretty lace curtains framing the windows of the dining room. A white tablecloth lay on the dining table, surrounded by intricately carved high-backed wooden chairs. Small houseplants decorated the window ledges—all reluctantly left behind by the homeowners in their chaotic haste to comply with a sudden eviction order.

The house was large enough to provide each girl with a private bedroom. As a child growing up in her grandparents' home in Vienna, her "bedroom" had been a couch in the living room, and there was little privacy in her subsequent home in Berlin. Since staying in crowded refugee camps, cramped quarters in the homes of strangers, and a dormitory at the Schlüterhof, her private bedroom at Ganzenmüllerstraße 33 was luxury that Tilly relished. She arranged her twin bed and nightstand with a reading lamp to the left of a tall window. A table and chair were in the middle of the room, where she spread her watercolors and paper to paint or draw. This small room became her sanctuary, where she dreamed and made plans for the future. The large backyard boasted a vegetable garden and a thick green lawn on which the girls picnicked on warm, sunny days. *Hausmeister* Pirkl always found stray animals who needed a home, so the girls cuddled with the various cats and dogs that lounged in the backyard.

On her first day at work, an officer briefed her on the relevant squadron regulations and work hours. Her job was simple enough: every morning, she and the other girls would walk up the street to Ganzenmüllerstraße 29 to sweep, dust, scrub, mop, change linens, make beds, and sew any rips in the bedding. A sewing machine was available in one of the rooms, which she happily used for her own needs; she was an excellent tailor. Because materials were scarce, she had to get by with what she could find. Tilly recalled, "When I worked as a housekeeper for the Army Air Corps in Freising, the officers gave German help those wool olive drab blankets, which were heavy but warm. I had one dyed black and made a serviceable winter suit out of it to wear. It was okay; nobody had fancy clothes. We all made do—a good habit."

Tilly poses with a Rolleicord camera.[4]

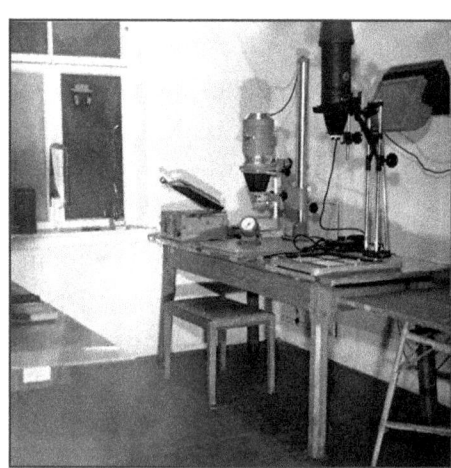

Photo developing room at the BOQ.

To celebrate obtaining another job with the Americans that included housing benefits, Tilly fulfilled her dream of owning a high-quality camera by purchasing a German-made Rolleicord from a shop in Freising. In exchange for modeling in an advertisement promoting the shop owner's new Rollei cameras, he gave Tilly a discount on her purchase. A twin-lens reflex camera, the Rollicord used 120-type film, capturing twelve square images on each roll. Advanced features included rapid shutter speeds and a fast sync speed for flash photography. Tilly was often seen with her Rolleicord, and the officers grew so at ease in her company that they accepted her as the base amateur photographer. Several officers were also keen photographers and enjoyed collaborating with Tilly as they all sought the perfect candid shots. Their friendly little group was so enthusiastic that the officers set up a photo-developing darkroom in the BOQ.

From left: Lt. Farriss, Mrs. and Lt. Roger Haan, Mrs. and Maj. William McCormick, Lt. Col. Bob Cunningham, Berta Henne at the 604th, 1946.

A few of the officers' wives arrived in Freising, and the squadron sought additional housing to accommodate military families. To the relief of Freising's lord mayor, in October 1946, enlisted men and noncommissioned officers with the 604th were relocated from the city's hotel rooms and residences to reconditioned rooms in a newly created U.S. Army Air Corps base located on the site of a former Wehrmacht barracks, named the *Ersatz* or E Kaserne. One of three former Wehrmacht barracks in Freising either built or expanded in the 1930s, the E Kaserne was located at the north end of Prinz Ludwig Straße, near the Vimy Kaserne and the General von Stein Kaserne.[5] After the war, the U.S. military took control of all three barracks to house troops while retaining possession of requisitioned houses.

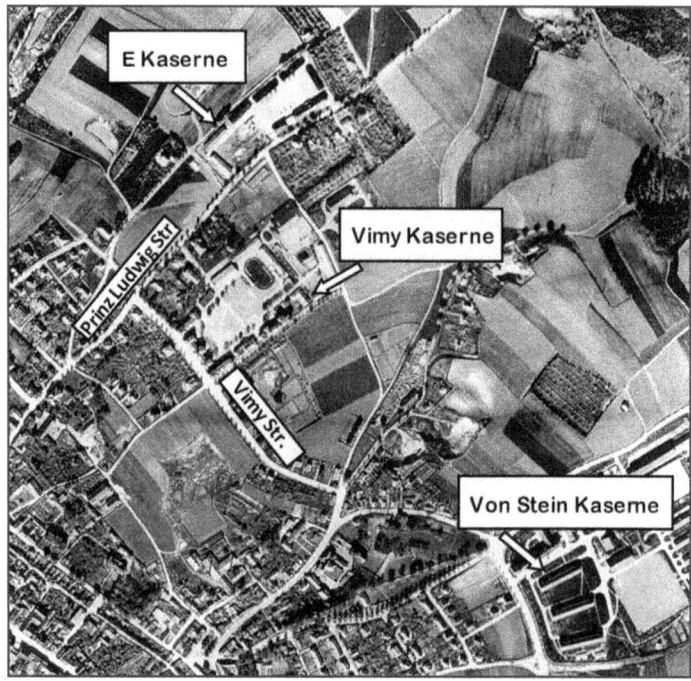

Aerial photo of Freising showing *Kasernes*, 1945.[6]

Billets and mess for the 604th men at E Kaserne.[7]

Maj. McCormick, Freising, 1946.

Tilly performed her duties well and adhered to the decorum expected of German civilians by the commanding officer (CO) of the squadron, Major William A. McCormick, Jr., an imposing man with an impressive background. She learned he had flown seventy-seven missions as a fighter pilot. He was shot down behind enemy lines, evaded capture, and rejoined American troops. Among other honors, he was awarded the Distinguished Flying Cross for his bravery.

A tidied room belonging to an officer in the BOQ at Ganzenmüllerstraße 29.

As the days passed, she got to know the officers whose rooms she tidied. They treated her kindly, and she enjoyed brightening their rooms with little bunches of flowers retrieved from the garden. She listened intently as they talked about the history, mission, and operations of the 604th.

The U.S. Army's Tactical Control Squadrons originated in the Army Signal Corps during the war. Composed of Signal Corps technicians who operated and maintained highly technical equipment and experienced Air Corps pilots, or "controllers," who guided flight interceptors, the 555th Signal Aircraft Warning Battalion's companies used radar and radio detection finding (DF) units to locate and follow aircraft. Very high-frequency (VHF) relay stations facilitated two-way communications between the Signal Corps technicians and pilots of fighters and bombers, giving early warning of approaching hostile aircraft and directing Allied aircraft to enemy targets.[8]

After the war, the 555th Signal Aircraft Warning Battalion was converted from a Signal Corps to an Air Corps unit in the U.S. Army. It was designated as the 501st Tactical Control Group under the 12th Tactical Air Command, and its companies were renamed the 601st, 602nd, 603rd, and 604th Tactical Control Squadrons. The 604th became one of four radar and VHF/DF units strategically located in the American zone with the mission to detect and track aircraft and provide advance notice of developing weather systems.[9] Allied pilots flying supplies or personnel through the area used the radio call sign "Racecard" to contact the 604th for information and navigational aid.

**VHF fixer coverage provided by squadrons in the 501st Tactical Control Group, 1946.**[10]

The 604th had a big job to do when they rolled into Freising in the dead of winter. The first task was to set up the SCR-527 (Signal Corps Radio model 527),[11] which was a medium-range radar used for early warning and ground-controlled interception of aircraft. The squadron located the radar site a few kilometers out of town to ensure the best control of the area assigned to it. A VHF/DF station was established at a second location, about a quarter kilometer from the radar site. This station was part of a network across the Western occupation zones known as the "fixer net," which monitored and controlled radio communications and broadcast weather advisories. Used in conjunction with the radar sites, the VHF/DF stations increased aircraft detection and communication capabilities.[12]

Integrated wires and radio circuits connected the radar site and VHF/DF station to an information center.[13] At the information center, operators tracked incoming aircraft on oscilloscope screens. Controllers collaborated with the operators, providing critical air experience and knowledge while communicating with the approaching pilot. In other words, the controllers spoke "Air Force" in a Signal Corps unit. The men in the information center plotted continuous bearings of aircraft radio emissions on a board to track the aircraft's flight, enabling controllers to guide the pilot.[14]

**The 604th's radar site, Freising, 1948.**[15]

Typically, a tactical control squadron was commanded by a lieutenant colonel or major, assisted by at least ten officers who were controllers at the captain or lieutenant rank, and supported by a hundred or more enlisted men.[16] At the time of

Tilly's hire, the squadron was acutely understaffed, consisting of only eight officers and eighty-four enlisted men.[17] German men and women were needed to augment staff as manual, kitchen, and cleaning laborers, especially since facility repairs and expansions were ongoing.

She watched men pass in and out of the base due to reenlistment furloughs, completion of service, transfers, temporary duty assignments, emergency leaves, dependency discharges, and redeployments. The replacements kept the place abuzz with new introductions, on-the-fly training, and fresh faces with new stories. Frequent personnel changes caused disruption, prompting the unit historian to complain, "Men lost included most of the key personnel and replacements will require a long time to achieve their know-how in the various jobs."[18] An unpredictable drop in controllers rotating out was the biggest concern. The base was on the verge of closing in June before more officers were sent.

**From left: Lt. Bell, Lt. Farriss and Capt. Busher, and Lt. Byars and Kavanaugh with unknown women.**

New officers who arrived at the 604th in June included 1st Lieutenant Jack Kavanaugh, 2nd Lieutenant Dale van Cleave, and 2nd Lieutenant Roger Haan, accompanied by his wife. Other officers rotating through the base that summer included lieutenants Frank A. Bell, Kenneth Smith, Orten H. Chappell, Nicholas R. Apone, Alvin N. Jutz, Byars, Farriss, Thompson, and Browning, as well as Captains George J. Busher and Reas. Lieutenant Colonel Bob Cunningham arrived to relieve Major MacCormick.

**From left: Lt. Chappell, Capt. Reas, Lt. Smith, Lt. Browning.**

**From left: Lt. van Cleave, Lt. Apone, Shorty and Lt. Thompson, and Lt. Jutz**

**Lt. Col. Cunningham and Tilly.[19]**

The 604th had inherited "frail and ailing" equipment that provoked frequent complaints among the men: "The equipment is old and gives trouble continually." First Lieutenant Green commented, "The radar coasting along on its reputation finally succumbed to old age and went off the air for several days while major repairs were made. . ... How much longer this veteran of the war will be able to last is extremely problematic."[20] Wartime shortages persisted in the postwar era, which meant that the squadron had to wait to receive new equipment. In the meantime, the men focused on making repairs. Despite being overworked, the men's morale was high, and their good-natured laughter made Tilly enjoy her time working for the officers.

While curious to explore the opportunities in her new situation, she worried about her family. She had sent letters to her relatives to let them know she was in Freising. Slowly, the network of letters circulated to family members, each sharing whatever news of the others they received. Cousin Clara, who lived in California, became a lifeline to her German family in the years to come.

One of the first postcards Tilly received was from her great aunt Luise, who lived in Leipzig in the Soviet zone. Dated September 25, 1946, Luise's note asked Tilly to act as an intermediary between her and Clara because "in the Russian occupied area, it is unsafe to send mail to the U.S.A. Please write to Clara that censorship still exists." Luise feared Russian censorship about her news of hunger in Soviet occupied eastern Germany. The food supply was low in quantity and quality throughout all of Germany.

As the specter of malnutrition hovered over postwar Europe (later referred to as *Der Hungerwinter* of 1946–1947), leaders of various American private non-profit charities banded together to form "Cooperative for American Remittances to Europe" or CARE. The mission of CARE was to provide food assistance through packages. The first shipments to Europe arrived in May 1946, and reached Germany by August 1946, bringing welcome assistance to ten European countries by the end of the year. The boxes contained meat, lard, fruit preserves, chocolate, milk and egg powders, and coffee.[21] Food companies joined the endeavor, and then the American public wanted to become CARE sponsors, including Tilly's American cousins. Despite ongoing worries at the end of 1946, Tilly found enough blessings to give her hope for a brighter future.

Tilly's message on her photo of the Schlüterhof at Christmas, 1946.

Early 1947 brought dramatic developments for Tilly, her family, and the base. She watched the food crisis worsen, with farmers around Munich delivering less than 40 percent of their grain quotas and the population suffering from cold due to fuel shortages. The future of Bavaria looked grim.[22] The Reichsmark had completely lost its value, and the people were frustrated with the high prices on the black market. The possibility of an organized and efficient self-governing Germany looked distant. Tilly's admiration for, and friendships with, the American military personnel she worked with inspired her to embrace the American way of life. She resolved to emigrate to America, where she believed her future held the brightest possibilities. Her previous decisions had been forced by life-threatening circumstances—escaping from Berlin, fleeing Thalheim, and migrating to Freising—and every decision had changed her destiny in unforeseeable ways. However, her decision to emigrate was made on her own terms, as a single woman. Many German women found themselves alone at the close of the war, so Tilly was not unique in confronting the future without a man by her side. While more than 14,000 German women chose to become American GI war brides during the first five years after the war,[23] Tilly did not center her identity around being a wife, dependent on a husband for her well-being. Although she desired love, she was not yet willing to sacrifice her independence.

Confidently and bravely, Tilly set about initiating her quest. A critical first step was to save enough money for the cost of transportation to the United States, and she knew this would take time. In March 1947, she reached for pen and paper to write a letter to Clara in California. In the letter, she declared her desire to emigrate and asked for Clara's help. Tilly received Clara's reply a month later:

> We note that you have so far led a very interesting life, and from the hardships have become very self-sufficient. That, and moral integrity combine to make a very good

citizen, such as any country needs. If you wish to come to America to be a moral, self-sufficient citizen, I would be willing to assist you financially and vouch for your character. We could take care of you here until you found a position, and from there you could work your way up in any field, as you attained money and experience. Not many German citizens are being admitted, but many Jews. Relay the requirements to me and I can do what is necessary on this side. So far, only very close relatives are being given the preferences [for emigrating]. ...I admire you for wishing to change your life for the better. I do not believe there are many Germans in San Diego... I believe the antagonisms engendered by the frightful war have subsided and the intelligent American is traditionally tolerant.

Meanwhile, the meager food supply in 1947 was devastating her family's health. Tilly shouldered the responsibility of relaying communications sent in letters between family members. In a letter to Tilly dated May 14, 1947, Clara wrote about her attempts to get a CARE package to Aunt Luise in Leipzig.

> All efforts to get packages into Leipzig have failed so far. The money sent to Aunt Luise was returned from CARE. No one has received an answer saying they received anything. We are having a hard time getting supplies to relatives in Leipzig and receiving communications from them. I sympathize deeply with you and all our kinfolk in all their suffering.

In the effort to help relatives in Leipzig, Tilly heard from her cousin Gladys, who also lived in California. Gladys wrote, "I finally heard from Luise. They have told me of the great food shortage. I packed some food and clothing to send. It makes us feel badly that they are suffering, and we must surely want to help them as much as possible." Unfortunately, by the time a CARE package was delivered to Luise in Leipzig, she had died. Also living under Soviet occupation were her grandparents in Vienna, who wrote her a letter about their situation dated May 19, 1947. Although they tried to make light of their hardships, they noted,

> It is very sad that we cannot be together for a long time. It is quite dreadful that Bavaria, too, is closed. How long will that last? Are not even the closest relatives allowed to find each other? I am lucky to have survived the war without any damage to myself or the house. I'm still in the best of health, which could not even be affected by the last cold winter, although I stayed in bed for three months because my small room could seldom be warmed from 5 to 8°C and rarely up to 12°C. [He could not obtain coal and wood for heat]. I'm quite sensitive to the cold. You are obviously well, apart from the long work hours, at least better than many others that don't find any work and still must feel hunger. We have enough to eat as we have many visitors from the countryside [relatives bring food from farms]. Otherwise, we would be hungry. Your poor people in Berlin, your mom, I'm very sorry for them. In Berlin, it looks too sad. If only one could send them parcels. . . Although it is hard

from here to judge your present situation correctly, I still believe that you could stay [in Germany] and that after the withdrawal of the Occupying Powers something similar [to your present job] could be sought. I am very satisfied with your independent character, which lets us hope that nothing can get you down. When the borders are opened, we want to be together immediately.

While the Germans were busy addressing the severe food crisis gripping their land, the U.S. Strategic Air Forces in Europe began to demobilize, doggedly following directives for severe budget cuts in the immediate postwar era when balancing the federal budget was a priority. The plan was to only keep enough aircraft and personnel in Germany for communication and transport.[24] Reductions preceded a confusing series of name and organizational changes that suggested the army couldn't decide what to do with the Air Corps units. The first change was the transfer of the four tactical control squadrons to the command of the renamed U.S. Air Forces in Europe, headquartered at Wiesbaden Air Base. The second change was inactivation of the 501st Group Battalion at Bad Kissingen and the 603rd Tactical Control Squadron at Neustadt. This left three tactical control squadrons manning radar sites at Rothwesten, Darmstadt, and Freising, now under the control of the 51st Troop Carrier Wing.

As the Army Air Corps implemented budget cuts and organizational changes, a few insightful military leaders monitored the developing Communist threat to governments in eastern Europe. They were alarmed by the Soviet policy of aggressively exporting communism through military aid, economic assistance, and coercion. By mid-1947, rising tensions and deteriorating relations marked the onset of the Cold War.[25] To address their concerns, leaders, including General Curtis E. LeMay, proposed an air force independent from the army to strengthen the security of the United States. The increasing role of aviation during both world wars and the dawning of the Cold War had expanded and advanced the Army Air Corps mission to the point of its being a separate service branch in need of its own allocation of military assets. In September 1947, Congress agreed it was time to restructure the military and passed the National Security Act, which created the Department of the Air Force (USAF).[26] Five months later, a significant Cold War crisis developed and the newly formed USAF in Europe came to regret the short-sighted cutbacks in aircraft, airmen, and radar coverage.

## Chapter 6. Charting a Different Path

In late 1947, visions of a future Germany sharply differed between the United States and the Soviet Union. While the United States and its allies aimed to rebuild West Germany as a capitalistic country with an independent and democratically led government, the Soviets schemed to develop a socialist country in East Germany under centralized communist rule. Halting the spread of communism became a prime concern of the U.S Government, precipitating two major changes in American military policy: the U.S. began to consider Germany as an ally combating communism, and the USAF prepared to defend air bases against hostile aircraft approaching from the Soviet bloc by establishing a warning system. The original mission of the 604th—to provide navigational aid and furnish weather information for all military aircraft operating in the area—was expanded in November 1947 to form a link in the aircraft warning system in Europe for defensive and offensive purposes.[1]

By this time, the 604th had grown in strength to sixteen officers, 215 enlisted men, and 137 indigenous civilians, with Major Lloyd C.E. Urquhart in command. Not only did Tilly have more rooms to clean, but her work became harder as medical personnel emphasized "immaculate, dust-free billets to reduce and keep to a minimum the possibility of respiratory illness."[2] As she spent more time in the BOQ, she became acquainted with the new officers who had transferred into the 604th, including first lieutenants Charles E. Byrne, George A. Cox, Grady F. Davenport, James D. Eastham, John T. Honeywell, Matthew J. Quilter, Doc Kapnick, Lura E. Hearn, and Hamilton. With new personnel rotating into the 604th on a regular basis, Lt. Cox was placed in charge of training the incoming soldiers in radar operations.

From left: Lt. Davenport, Lt. Eastham, and Lt. Quilter.

From left: Lt. Hearn, Lt. Byrne, and Lt. Cox.

From left: Maj. Urquhart,[3] Lt. Kapnick, Lt, Hamilton, and Lt. Honeywell.

Lt. Cox's men after graduating from radar operations school at the 604th.

With the 604th fully staffed, the army tasked the unit with a democratization program called German Youth Activities (GYA).[4] The army used the GYA to target German youth who had grown up absorbing Nazi ideas. The army wanted these young people off the streets and engaged in craft and athletic activities similar to those enjoyed by youth in the United States. The army's aim was to reduce juvenile delinquency stemming from idleness and to redirect any militaristic or nationalistic tendencies toward democratic ideals.[5] Many American soldiers readily volunteered to supply craft supplies and sports equipment, and sponsor parties and competitions for German girls and boys. While having fun, German youths learned democratic values such as fair play and teamwork. American swing music attracted youths to GYA dances, where the lively music helped relieve stress and bring smiles. The young people mingled with friends at the dances, chatted with Americans, ate snacks, and momentarily forgot past traumas.[6]

On Thanksgiving Day, the officer in charge of the Freising district's GYA program, Lt. Davenport, invited Tilly to help the 604th host German children from the local orphanage. The children were served food far beyond their usual rations and given chocolate and fruit afterward. Tilly was amazed at the generosity of the men and their efforts to make the children feel welcome, reinforcing her admiration for Americans.

\*\*\*

At the end of November, two fighter aircraft, the P-47 and P-51, became available to pilots at the 604th to practice interceptions of potentially hostile aircraft coming from the Soviet bloc. Collecting and transmitting information on potentially hostile aircraft was key to effective interceptions and provided valuable experience to the radar crews. After the aircraft was located and its altitude resolved, crews passed the information to a command center. If the commander deemed the aircraft was a threat, he directed interceptor aircraft to scramble. The operations crew in the information center then vectored the interceptor to the target.[7]

Tilly photographed the pilots as they prepared for their daily flight maneuvers. She watched the fliers, easy and sure of themselves, charging their ships with power, then picking up speed before carefully lifting tons of metal off the runway into the sky. After a tiring day immersed in the elements, flying with concentrated tension as they scanned for possible threats, the officers found relief at their club, the "20 MPH," where they regaled listeners with their airborne adventures.

Their status as aviators gave them prestige, and when the officers occasionally invited the *Mädels* from Ganzenmüllerstraße to brighten the club with their companionship, they gladly accepted.

**From left: Lts. Quilter, Davenport, and Cox on an early morning at the airport.**

**Behind the bar from left: Capt. Busher, Berta, Lt. Browning at the 20 MPH club, 1948 (women on ends are unknown).**

**Maj. McCary and Lt. Eastham (right) laugh with others (unknown) at the 20 MPH club, 1949.**

All the pilots had seen action in the war, and Tilly listened as they recounted the dangers while laughing with the joy of having survived. The club was an asylum for the pilots, a place to slake their thirst and sit in the company of their fellows, bound by shared experiences. Along with telling stories, several pilots shared photos of their missions with Tilly. Her fascination with the photos was tainted with distress from her war memories, but still, Tilly warmed to her friends' stirring accounts of unforeseen pitfalls in fearsome weather and their encounters with landscapes of breathtaking beauty.

**Lt. Cox in a B-17 facing flak; photo taken from the right waist gunner position.**[8]

**Lt. Eastham in a P-51D.**

**A P-47 flown by Lt. Davenport.**[9]

Lt. Cox described piloting his B-17 Flying Fortress past snow-peaked crags and into valleys patchworked with myriad earthly colors. Sighting enemy fighters coming up fast, the right-waist gunner had unleashed a torrent of bullets. Lt. Eastham, who flew P-51 Mustangs with the 55th and 31st Fighter Groups during the war, related stories of escorting bombers while maneuvering through antiaircraft fire. Lt. Davenport, a twenty-five-year-old whose fresh face belied his 104 combat missions during the war, flew a P-47 Thunderbolt with such heroism that he received the Distinguished Flying Cross. The stories thrilled with excitement, and it was not surprising that the young women thought of the aviators as bold heroes.

As 1947 came to a close, the men of the 604th found time to plan a Christmas party for the children of Freising's orphanage. The Christmas party was a gesture of American goodwill toward a community still overcoming the consequences of war. The officers' wives and enlisted men raised donations for supplies, and the USAF donated fifteen cases of candy. Tilly and other German civilians worked with the men to make decorations and prepare gifts. The squadron's historian recounted the event in the monthly report.[10]

> The program consisted of a song fest, a play conducted by the children, a film entitled '*Der Kleine Muck*,' followed by the distribution of candy. It was necessary to hold the program three times to accommodate the 2,500 orphans. All the little children had a good time. Santa Claus was present throughout the entire program. Later, a dance and party were held for teenagers aged fourteen and older. Approximately 250 took part in this affair.

The year 1948 brought fast-developing and far-reaching changes to Western Europe's political, economic, and military landscape. In February, the U.S. government was shocked when the Communist Party in Czechoslovakia, with Soviet support, staged a coup, solidifying Eastern Europe as a communist bloc. The event dealt a deathblow to the relations between the two superpowers. Realizing that a prosperous Western Europe would deter the spread of communism and become a thriving trading partner, Congress approved the Marshall Plan in April. This plan allocated billions of dollars to aid Germany in tackling the prolonged food crisis, rebuilding destroyed infrastructure, and modernizing industry. There was a growing belief that Germany's economic recovery was crucial to the well-being of Europe.[11]

By early summer 1948, the food situation had improved dramatically, and an excellent harvest was in the forecast.[12,13] With more food and the Marshall Plan funds flowing in, people living in the western zones of Germany foresaw better times ahead, and their spirits brightened. In another sign of progress, the integration of dislocated civilians into the socioeconomic fabric of Freising, while still faced with challenges, had been aided by the refugees' strong motivation and technical skills. More than 200 successful "refugee camp companies" had been established, producing high-quality goods and employing hundreds of workers.[14]

The men at the 604th were happy to learn that the 603rd had been reactivated and stationed at Hof, bringing back four tactical control squadrons to staff radar installations in the American zone.[15] Everyone was in high spirits. The 604th was at a healthy staffing level of 370, including 111 indigenous civilians. The addition of Captain Donald F. Flaharty brought the number of squadron officers to nineteen. The sky was bustling with traffic, with the 604th giving navigational aid to 1,200–1,500 aircraft per month. In their spare time, the airmen enthusiastically engaged in recreational activities, forming teams and organizing games for basketball, volleyball, baseball, tennis, and golf. During downtime, the men goofed around, played with their dogs, and pursued hobbies such as photography and model trains. As Tilly photographed the men enjoying leisure activities, she sensed that these escapes from their routine challenges eased their worries and stress about being far from home.

**Lt. Busher with a model train.**

**"Convicted!" Lt. Eastham and Lt. Quilter goofing around.**

**Tennis at the 604th.**

**Lt. Byrne and Butch.**

Capt. Flaharty and his dog, George.

Lt. Cox and Heinz.

Three years had passed since the end of the war, and Tilly's trauma had transformed into a zest for enjoying the things in life that she had been deprived of. She was strong and self-reliant yet exceedingly vulnerable. She had no experience dating men. German men aged sixteen to sixty had been drafted to fight in the war, and the casualty rate was so high that women far outnumbered men.[16] After the war, most of the remaining German men were either in prisoner-of-war camps or broken and weary. In contrast, the American soldiers were well-fed, handsome fellows with good-natured smiles and a casual, confident bearing that appealed to young German women.

With her photo buddies, Lts. Cox, Quilter, and Eastham, she formed untroubled friendships. They'd sometimes clown around and tease her, but it was lighthearted fun that did not overstep her comfort level, and she enjoyed their attention. Their mutual interest in camera advancements, lenses, photo lighting, and composition provoked lively conversations that erased their cultural differences. The Nazi past felt distant as Tilly embraced the victors and all that they stood for.

Reflecting in later years, she exclaimed, "It was the happiest time of my life!"

But some officers, accustomed to wielding power and authority over others, used their prestige and charm to seek self-gratification. One lieutenant, in particular, exploited Tilly's naiveté and inexperience with a warm smile in carefully controlled moments of isolation. Alone in the sewing room, as she sat pumping the foot-operated treadle, he would stand close, talking softly. She could feel the warmth of his hands as they gently caressed her shoulders. On her days in the sewing room, she began to look for his shadow crossing the doorway, wondering if she would see him. Seeking validation of her attractiveness, she was flattered by his attention and looked forward to his visits.

One day, after she finished her sewing task and stood up, he turned her toward him, brushing his lips across her cheek. He wore perfectly calm self-assurance while she trembled with shy pleasure. Tilly had relied on herself for a long time and had trusted her feelings, but her emotions were unguided, and trusting her feelings did not always serve her well. Deftly manipulated by her seducer, she imagined romance, and like most victims, was blind to the true intentions behind his pursuit. She needed to be loved and valued but did not know that she had entrusted her heart to someone without a conscience.

Their affair was brief; airmen did not remain in one place for long. She found out later that he was married. It took her some time to recognize that she had been fooled; it was too painful to believe that someone she trusted and cared about had lied to her. Reckoning with her vulnerability, she resolved to become wiser.

***

In June, historic events disrupted the convivial mood on base. First, the Western Allies replaced the worthless Nazi-era Reichsmark with the new Deutschmark to stabilize the economy in western occupation zones. The Deutschmark hit the streets on June 20, 1948, surprising everyone. Second, on the same day, rationing and price controls were lifted on most goods except food. Seemingly overnight, these two actions solved the economic problems plaguing communities: shortages and black-market activity.[17]

The sudden appearance of the Deutschmark caught the Soviets off guard. Enraged that currency reform had secretly occurred without their involvement and was only for the western-occupied zones, they retaliated on June 24 by blocking all land, river, and rail traffic into the three Allied sectors comprising West Berlin, Germany's isolated capital city deeply embedded in communist-controlled territory. The Soviets intended to forcefully consolidate the city under their political and economic control. In a severe lack of foresight, however, their plan to capture West Berlin through starvation did not include the closure of air corridors servicing the city's airports. The Soviets simply didn't believe that the two million people living in West Berlin could be kept alive through air transport alone.[18]

To Clay and other high-ranking American officials, West Berlin was a symbol of American resolve for the future of Europe, and to abandon the city would severely damage U.S. credibility. Clay called LeMay, commander of the newly created USAF in Europe, and asked if his planes could conduct an airlift of emergency supplies into the city. LeMay replied, "Sir, the Air Force can deliver anything."[19] LeMay's logistics staff calculated that 1,439 tons of food and 2,000 tons of coal were needed each day to supply the basic needs of the city's residents. However, there was nowhere near the number of aircraft in Europe to meet this level of demand. LeMay ordered the large Douglas C-54 Skymasters, planes capable of hauling 10 tons, to be flown in from locations worldwide to two main staging sites for the airlift—the Wiesbaden and Rhein-Mann Air Force bases. Until the Skymasters arrived, LeMay ordered all Douglas C-47 Skytrains, planes capable of hauling 3 tons, along with their pilots and crews stationed in Europe, to report to the staging sites for the round-the-clock mission of flying supplies into West Berlin.

On June 26, 1948, a combined task force of American and British troops was formed to airlift supplies into West Berlin and placed under the command of USAF Major General William H. Tunner.[20] The mission was codenamed "Operation Vittles."[21] The West Berliners knew that their newly acquired freedom and welfare depended on everyone's combined efforts—solidarity was needed to foil the communist takeover of their beloved city. In a dawning realization, West Berliners began to see the enemy who bombed them yesterday as the friend who worked to save them today.

The 604th was called upon to provide airlift personnel. Under the new command of Lieutenant Colonel Fred J. Collins, a steady stream of pilots from the 604th were transferred to the airlift, with newcomers Capt. Aloys W. Fuessel, Jr. and Lt. Orville D. Coil, along with Lts. Cox, Byrne, and Quilter making runs in July. As the summer progressed, Capt. Frank W. Schlabs joined the aerial resupply mission. Tilly's friend, Lt. Eastham, entered this massive humanitarian undertaking in August 1948.[22]

**Lt. Col. Collins.**

**From left: Capt. Fuessel, Lt. Coil, and Capt. Schlabs.**

Attached to the 60th Troop Carrier Group at Wiesbaden, Eastham relieved exhausted pilots flying C-47s virtually nonstop.[23,24] Ironically, five years earlier, he had flown with the 55th Fighter Group, escorting B-17 bombers intent on destroying the Germans.[25] Now, he found himself defending them against a former ally by delivering food aid and, through this effort, reshape German memory of the war with a symbol of man's humanity to man—the *Berliner Luftbrücke*.

Eastham later recounted his flights into West Berlin to his companions at the 20 MPH Club. He flew a prescribed 435-km path to the Tempelhof Airport in West Berlin at an altitude of 5,500 feet, flying at 170 mph, and 3 minutes behind the plane in front of him. He followed beacons from ground radar stations that guided his path to Fulda, the last checkpoint before entering airspace above the Russian occupation zone. Here, he turned to a heading of 057 degrees, entered the 32-kilometer-wide air corridor, radioed into Tempelhof, and waited for the ground-controlled approach (GCA) operator to give him landing instructions. If pilots veered off course, the GCA operator would vector them to the correct heading. One indicator that they were too close to the corridor's edge was the sudden appearance of Russian fighters.[26] Pilots could complete two to three roundtrips during each 12-hour shift.[27] They flew seven days a week, regardless of the weather.

Berlin was notorious for poor weather, which could be zero-zero (very low ceiling and visibility), even in summer. Eastham would encounter rain, fog, hail, or snow flurries on one flight! They flew in all weather. Heavy fog? Iced planes? No matter, they flew anyway. Every trip was an instrument flight. The tricky part about landing at Tempelhof was maneuvering the descent to avoid seven-story apartment buildings lining both sides of the runway. Despite bad weather and tight clearance, GCA operators had planes stacked in altitude and staggered in distance, landing every 3 minutes. A pilot had one shot at landing, and if he missed the approach, he couldn't reenter the congested pattern but instead had to go back to base loaded.[28]

Eastham's loads varied from dehydrated potatoes, powdered eggs and milk, flour, coffee, macaroni, and clothes. Coal was stuffed into duffel bags to prevent coal dust from suffocating the crew and corroding the electrical components of the plane. On many flights, CARE packages were also included in the cargo.²⁹ Chocolate bars and gum, bundled into handkerchiefs and dropped by the crew in approaching planes to children waiting at the edge of runways, became a special treat for the youngsters of West Berlin, a tradition begun by airlift pilot Lieutenant Gail S. Halvorson.³⁰ The larger C-54 Skymasters began to arrive to replace the C-47s, which were relieved from duty along with their pilots. Eastham returned to the 604th as an interceptor controller.

\*\*\*

Tilly worried about her family in West Berlin. Even before the blockade, people suffered from hunger. Was her family able to get enough food and essential items through the airlift? She had no way of knowing that her family, along with millions of other Berliners, would have to endure eleven months of the blockade. To think of her family struggling was disheartening. Christel was ten years old during the blockade and later recalled, "The airlift was wonderful and helped a lot. At school, they gave us a warm soup delivered every day by the planes. We took this soup to the children who were sick at home in bed."

At the end of September, 1948, Tilly mailed her emigration application to the Consulate General in Munich. Upon receipt of the application, the consulate assigned her a number and told her to wait for further instructions. There was a quota on the number of Germans allowed to emigrate to the U.S., and Tilly had no idea if she would be accepted or how long she would have to wait. The waiting time would stretch into years, but when the consulate informed her, "It's your turn," she knew she would have to be ready. Thinking ahead, she asked

Lt. Cox to write her a letter of recommendation for her work at the 604th so she would have references for job hunting in America. In his letter dated October 24, 1948, he wrote,

> During Tilly's employment as housekeeper for the bachelor officers' quarters, she has proved to be outstandingly efficient, industrious, and entirely trustworthy. I have no hesitation in giving her an unqualified recommendation for character and industry. All officers occupying these quarters concur.

As she waited for her emigration application to be approved, the 604th continued to transform with new airmen and assignments. In December 1948, the squadron received orders redesignating the 604th as an Aircraft Control and Warning Squadron attached to the 7402nd Aircraft Control and Warning Group at Wiesbaden Air Base. With the Berlin Airlift ongoing and hostility with the Soviet Union increasing, the expanded mission of the 604th included surveillance and early warning service, intelligence missions, and controlling fighter aircraft for interception of hostile forces.

New emblem of the 604th.[31]

At Christmas, the commander of the 604th hosted a dinner for the squadron families and guests, as well as parties for the children of Freising. His message to the community was clear—America has the resources and commitment to help rebuild the country and will remain steadfast against communist aggressors threatening Germany's freedoms. America would not abandon the German people.

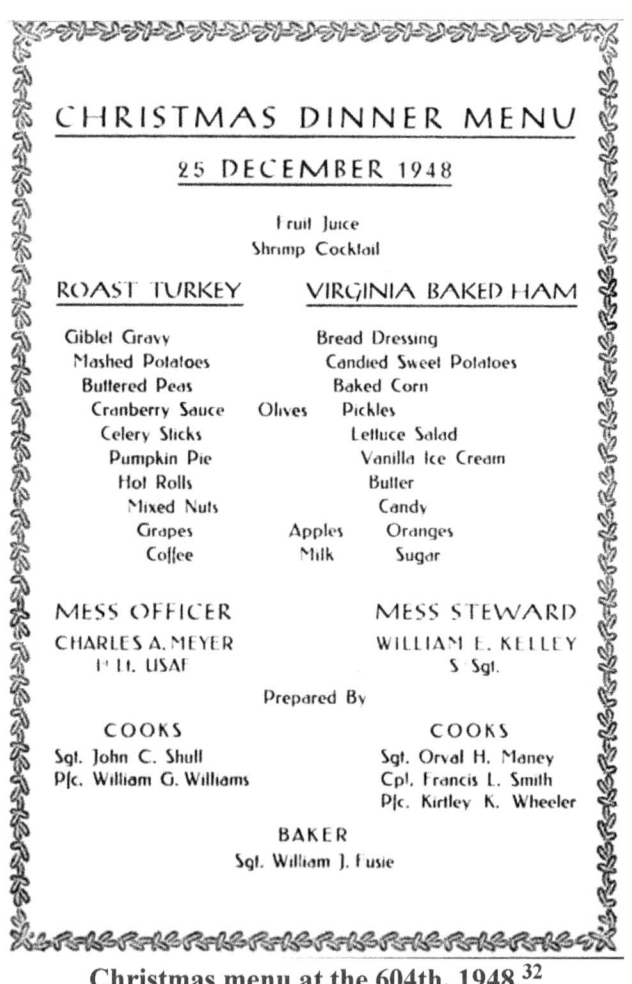

Christmas menu at the 604th, 1948.[32]

From December 19-23, 1948, the 604th hosted Christmas parties for more than 4,500 children in Freising, aged six to fourteen, and gave out gift packages containing candy, gum, and fruit. The squadron organized separate parties for orphans and refugee children, where they handed out clothing in addition to gift packages. On Christmas Day, squadron personnel served 210 meals in the mess hall and distributed souvenir menus.

With the dawn of 1949, significant changes occurred within the 604th. Eastham was transferred to the reactivated 36th Fighter Group at Fürstenfeldbruck Air Base, where he was assigned to pilot the Lockheed F-80 Shooting Star.[33] The jet fighters were intended to confront the growing threat posed by Soviet aircraft to the airlift.[34] The airlift was proceeding at full throttle. By April, pilots had set a record of 1,398 flights into West Berlin in 24 hours, with a plane landing on average every 61 seconds. Major James G. McCary arrived at the 604th to take over command from Lt. Col. Collins. Lts. Paul H. Hansen and Mike "Ralph" Reynolds also joined the squadron, while Tilly said goodbye to her departing photo buddies, who had been transferred to other bases.

**From left: Maj. McCary, Lt. Reynolds, and Lt. Hansen.**

**New gate and guard building at the 604th, 1949.**

Some of the changes she watched unfold exasperated the airmen but, from her point of view, had a comical side to them. The commander wanted to enhance the military atmosphere of the base, so a new guard building and gate were installed at the entrance. However, the men balked at orders to conform to the "School of the Soldier," training in military discipline and fitness. As members of a technical unit, the men were used to more relaxed attire and bearing than was required in combat units. To encourage the men's cooperation, the man with the "neatest appearance and most alert mind" was given a 24-hour pass. This system of bribery produced "gratifying" results. Another change was in the men's uniform. The new outfit had "violently contrasting colors of insignia and decoration that some men feel makes them look like hotel doormen."[35] The change that caused the most outrage was a command that military personnel replace all German cooks. The abrupt replacement resulted in complaints about the food.

The men didn't want to lose their German cooks! In a clever workaround to this unpopular policy, the men voluntarily contributed a small monthly sum to hire their German cooks back as assistants to military personnel.

Further reductions in civilian workers at air bases were ordered by the U.S. European Command shortly after the German cooks were dismissed. The number of civilians working at the 604th was reduced by 30 percent, leaving only sixty-eight. The loss of workers for maintenance, cleaning, and other duties proved a serious detriment to the 604th and caused acute problems for Major McCary. His solution was to instruct the remaining workers to be "more industrious,"[36] meaning they had to work harder and faster.

Tilly could see the writing on the wall. It was time to leave her job and life in Freising. Watching the constant changes around her, she sensed she was also changing. She was restless and no longer content with just the security of food and housing provided by the U.S. military. She had bigger dreams and looked forward to learning new skills, forming new connections, and exploring new surroundings. Over the past four years, while working for the Americans in Freising, she had matured from a girl of twenty to a woman of twenty-four. War experiences had shaped her, and while she would always carry them with her, she had discovered the confidence to live however she wanted.

In a sign of positive change on the horizon, the Soviets recognized the futility of blockading West Berlin and ended their siege on May 12, 1949.[37] In total, the airlift carried 2,325,510 tons of cargo, with coal comprising most of the load, followed by food and miscellaneous goods needed to keep the city running.[38] Shortly thereafter, the West German

Parliamentary Council convened and drafted a provisional constitution for what would become the Federal Republic of Germany, a democratic nation formed from the three western Allied zones of occupation. West Germany began its journey toward becoming an economic powerhouse with a free press and laws that protected individual liberties.

Tilly celebrates better times in 1949 with a new outfit.[39]

The Second World War had cost seven million German lives, and everyone had felt this devastating loss. With the promise of prosperity in a new democratic order, marriages and births that young couples had postponed due to hardship and uncertainty rebounded, thereby helping to replenish the population. Tilly captured scenes around her on film, preserving pictorial memories of people intent on rebuilding their lives and German society.

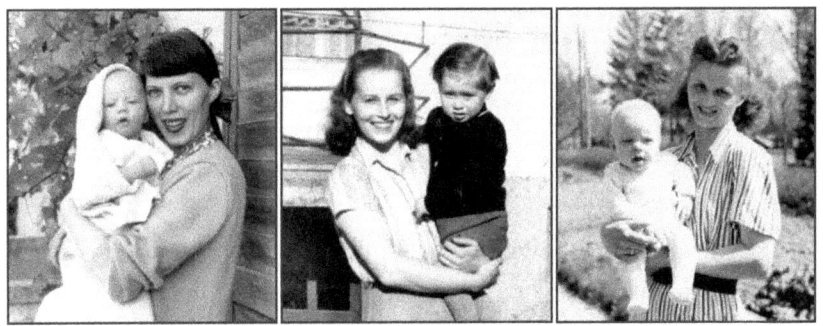

**From left: Timothy Lee and mother, Bertl and son Gernold, Frau Niemela and Peter, 1949.**

Anticipating communication from the American Consulate, she resigned from her job at the 604th in December. At the start of 1950, she moved back to Berlin to be with her dear mother once again. After so many years apart and after all they had been through, the brief moments they had left together were precious. On February 13, a letter arrived from an agent of the American Express Company stating that her travel to America had been authorized, and a place had been booked for her "in a four-bed cabin on the *SS Washington* for the price of $250. The ship will begin the Atlantic crossing from the port of Hamburg on April 4." Her anticipation of the journey to America was tinged with sadness as she contemplated leaving her family. While waiting to depart, she received heartfelt words from her uncle in Vienna.

> All of us wish you much good luck for this journey from all our hearts, and much happiness in your new way of life. May your heart's desire be fulfilled. We hope your good fortune will relieve the pain of goodbye and parting from your mother. We envy you quite a lot. Take the good and genuine

aspects of your German home country with you, there is much that even in the present situation we do not have to be ashamed of. So, do not forget—you will always remain one of ours.

Entirely on her own again, Tilly set out on a journey for an uncertain future, not knowing what risks lay ahead, but unlike her flight in 1945, her steps in 1950 were based on hope, not fear. She possessed the best qualities any young immigrant could offer a new country. On April 13, 1950, Tilly sighted the Statue of Liberty with feelings of intense emotion and sailed into New York to begin her new life in America.

**Tilly's first sight of the Statue of Liberty, April 13, 1950.**

# *References and Notes*

## Introduction

1. Earl Ziemke, *The U.S. Army in the Occupation of Germany 1944-1946*, Center of Military History, U.S. Army, Washington, D.C., 1975, p. 365.

General Lucius D. Clay, administrator of the Offices of the Military Government, United States, wrote in September, 1945, "The Potsdam Agreements call for restoration of local self-government as rapidly as consistent with the purposes of the occupation. If the Germans are to learn democracy, I think the best way is to start off quickly…"

## Prologue

1. *Berlin in the Air War*, Liberation Route Europe.
https://www.liberationroute.com/pois/258/berlin-in-the-air-war
Accessed July 20, 2024.

The February 3 mission was not Berlin's first aerial attack. Berliners received their first World War II aerial attack in 1940. Infrequent British and Soviet air attacks occurred in Berlin through 1942, inflicting little damage, but in 1943, British and American air forces teamed up for combined bomber offensives. The Royal Air Force area bombed at night, while the U.S. Army Air Forces conducted daytime precision attacks on military and industrial targets.

2. *Air War from 1939-1945*, American Experience, Public Broadcasting Service. https://www.pbs.org/wgbh/americanexperience/features/bombing-air-war-1939-1945/ Accessed July 14, 2024.

By the end of 1943, the combined bomber offensive had compromised Berlin's railways and rendered more than 25 percent of housing uninhabitable. In early 1944, the Royal Air Force and U.S. Army Air Forces launched intensive attacks on the capital city, named the Berlin Air Offensive. Thousands of tons of bombs blindly and indiscriminately battered everything from homes to munitions factories at a high cost of Allied planes and airmen. The Berlin Air Offensive destroyed 400,000 homes, killed thousands of civilians, and caused tens of thousands of homeless Berliners to flee the city. However, the bombing campaign failed to crucially damage critical infrastructure and did not elicit the surrender of Nazi Germany. For the remainder of 1944, most aerial attacks switched to France to support the ground invasion of Allied troops on D-Day.

3. Ibid.

4. Robert Dorr, *The Bombing of Berlin by Doolittle's Eighth Air Force*, Warfare History Network, 2014. https://warfarehistorynetwork.com/article/the-bombing-of-berlin-by-doolittles-eighth-air-force/ Accessed January 16, 2024.

5. *Berlin in the Air War*, Liberation Route Europe. https://www.liberationroute.com/pois/258/berlin-in-the-air-war Accessed July 20, 2024.

The initial Allied policy to attack only targets of direct military importance was abandoned early in the war after Hitler ordered an aerial attack on Rotterdam. Royal Air Force bomber commander Sir Arthur T. Harris firmly believed in the necessity of carpet-bombing cities to destroy infrastructure and housing and to demoralize the German people, regardless of civilian casualties.

6. Edward Westermann, *Flak: German Anti-Aircraft Defenses, 1914-1945*, University Press of Kansas, Lawrence, 2001, p. 1.

Large-scale German civilian deaths, while not a formal policy, were implied in Harris' wartime philosophy to "de-house" the German population and break their will to fight.

7. *Mission Date: February 3, 1945, Berlin, 100th Bomb Group Mission 255*, 100th Bomb Group Foundation.
https://100thbg.com/mission/?mission_id=290
Accessed July 5, 2024.

U.S. intelligence had reported that Germany's 6th Panzer Army was moving by train to meet the Russians at the Oder River and would pass through the Tempelhof railyards. (In reality, the report was wrong; no such movement occurred.) A forceful aerial assault to disrupt transportation and communication, damage infrastructure, and demoralize German civilians was essential for Allied unity. Additionally, targeting Berlin would force the Luftwaffe to defend the city, and the Americans anticipated the Germans would suffer heavy losses in the process.

8. James Doolittle and Carroll Glines, *I Could Never Be So Lucky Again*, Bantam Books, New York, 1991, p. 392.

9. *Mission 817: February 3, 1945*, American Air Museum in Britain. https://www.americanairmuseum.com/archive/mission/817
Accessed July 20, 2024.

10. *Crippling the Nazi War Machine: USAAF Strategic Bombing in Europe, Enabling Technologies*, National Museum of the United States Air Force, Wright-Patterson Air Force Base, Dayton, Ohio.
https://www.nationalmuseum.af.mil/Visit/Museum-Exhibits/Fact-Sheets/Display/Article/1506273/crippling-the-nazi-war-machine-usaaf-strategic-bombing-in-europe/ Accessed July 5, 2024.

While the B-17 could attain a higher ceiling and remain operational despite heavy damage, the faster B-24 had a longer range and could carry a heavier bomb load. Both bombers carried a crew of nine to ten airmen consisting of two pilots, a bombardier, a navigator, a radio operator/gunner, four gunners, and a toggler, who could fill in for the bombardier when needed to ensure the bombs were dropped on cue. Equipped with turbo-superchargers, the bombers could fly at 20,000 to 30,000 feet, making them less likely to be hit by flak from anti-aircraft guns.

11. *Crippling the Nazi War Machine: USAAF Strategic Bombing in Europe, Fighter Escort*, National Museum of the United States Air Force, Wright-Patterson Air Force Base, Dayton, Ohio. https://www.nationalmuseum.af.mil/Visit/Museum-Exhibits/Fact-Sheets/Display/Article/1506273/crippling-the-nazi-war-machine-usaaf-strategic-bombing-in-europe/ Accessed July 5, 2024.

At the start of the American involvement in the war, the USAAF did not have fighters to escort and protect bombers from attacks by German aces, resulting in high losses in bombers. While the bombers had machine guns to ward off German fighters, the enemy aircraft were equipped with rockets and cannons, making it easy to attack beyond the range of machine gun fire. It wasn't until 1943 that improvements in the range of American fighter aircraft allowed the USAAF to assign the P-47 Thunderbolt, the P-38 Lightning, and the P-51 Mustang as escorts to bombers. The fighter-bombers could also drop small but accurately aimed bombs.

12. John Correll, *Targeting the Luftwaffe*, Air and Space Forces Magazine, January 30, 2018. https://www.airandspaceforces.com/article/targeting-the-luftwaffe/ Accessed July 20, 2024.

Just days into his command of the 8th Air Force, Lieutenant General James D. Doolittle made a consequential change in air fighter strategy. Instead of holding close formations to protect bombers, the fighters were to fly ahead, hunt enemy aircraft, and destroy them where they found them. As the American fighters sought to engage and cripple the German aces mid-altitude, bombing runs became more effective with far fewer casualties while Luftwaffe losses accelerated.

13. Earl Beck, *Under the Bombs*, The University Press of Kentucky, Lexington, 1986, p. 48.

14. Ibid., p. 109.

15. Robert Dorr, *The Bombing of Berlin by Doolittle's Eighth Air Force*, Warfare History Network, 2014. https://warfarehistorynetwork.com/article/the-bombing-of-berlin-by-doolittles-eighth-air-force/ Accessed January 16, 2024.

The Nazis used fake airfields to divert bombing raids away from prime targets, dropped false smoke bombs to confuse Allied bomber crews into prematurely releasing their payload, and generated smoke to obscure ground targets. Acoustic locators, worn as a headset by Nazi gunners, detected the vibrations of Allied engines, giving early warnings of incoming aircraft.

16. *Crippling the Nazi War Machine: USAAF Strategic Bombing in Europe, Deadly Skies Over Europe*, National Museum of the United States Air Force, Wright-Patterson Air Force Base, Dayton, Ohio. https://www.nationalmuseum.af.mil/Visit/Museum-Exhibits/Fact-Sheets/Display/Article/1506273/crippling-the-nazi-war-machine-usaaf-strategic-bombing-in-europe/ Accessed July 5, 2024.

The German aerial defense relied on the nimble single-engine fighter, the Messerschmitt Bf 109, and the twin-engine destroyer, the Messerschmitt Bf 110. While the Luftwaffe faced shortages of experienced pilots and gasoline, on February 3, they still had 1,600 warplanes to defend the capital city of the Third Reich.

17. Herbert Vogt, *My Memories of Berlin: A Young Boy's Amazing Survival Story*, Xlibris Publishing, Bloomington, Indiana, 2012. p. 173.

Berlin was protected by over 100 small anti-aircraft batteries and three massive flak towers strategically placed to protect the city's center. Each tower had retractable radar, searchlights, and four twin anti-aircraft guns. A twin-gun mount weighed 26.5 tons and could fire a 62-pound shell at 2,800 feet per second, reaching 48,600 feet in altitude.

18. Ibid., p. 138 and 183.

The operation of flak guns was left to those unfit to serve in the Wehrmacht—boys, old men, and even girls. Males aged fourteen years and over were drafted to serve as *Flakhelfer*, assisting the adult load gunners and prisoners of war manning the anti-aircraft guns. By February 3, the fourteen-year-olds had been transferred to the Russian front and replaced by ten-year-olds.

19. USAAF Worldwide Operations Chronology, February 3, 1945, European Theater of Operations. https://aircrewremembered.com/USAAFCombatOperations/Feb.45.html Accessed July 14, 2024.

20. *Mission Date: February 3, 1945, Berlin, 100th Bomb Group Mission 255*, 100th Bomb Group Foundation. https://100thbg.com/mission/?mission_id=290 Accessed July 5, 2024.

21. Robert Dorr, *The Bombing of Berlin by Doolittle's Eighth Air Force*, Warfare History Network, 2014. https://warfarehistorynetwork.com/article/the-bombing-of-berlin-by-doolittles-eighth-air-force/ Accessed January 16, 2024.

22. Earl Beck, *Under the Bombs*, The University Press of Kentucky, Lexington, 1986, p. 86.

23. *Crippling the Nazi War Machine: USAAF Strategic Bombing in Europe*, National Museum of the United States Air Force, Wright-Patterson Air Force Base, Dayton, Ohio. https://www.nationalmuseum.af.mil/Visit/Museum-Exhibits/Fact-Sheets/Display/Article/1506273/crippling-the-nazi-war-machine-usaaf-strategic-bombing-in-europe/ Accessed July 5, 2024.

24. *Berlin in the Air War*, Liberation Route Europe. https://www.liberationroute.com/pois/258/berlin-in-the-air-war Accessed July 20, 2024.

# Chapter 1. Escape to an Uncertain Future

1. About AEG: 130 years of Reform and Innovation. https://www.aeg-imc.com/htm/en/aboutus.html Accessed January 14, 2024.

2. Barry Silverstein, *World War Brands: World War II and the Rise of the Modern American Brand*, Guide Words Publishing, Biltmore Lake, North Carolina, 2021, p. II.
AEG also supplied electrical power through transmission lines for buildings and transportation systems.

3. Jill Stephenson, *Women in Nazi Germany*, Routledge, New York, 2013, p. 8.

4. Claudia Koonz, *Mothers in the Fatherland: Women, the Family, and Nazi Politics*, Routledge, New York, 2013, p. 186.

5. Peter Hawkes and Martin Hÿtch, *The Beginnings of Electron Microscopy –Part 1*, Academic Press, London, 2021, p. 5–7.

6. A. Kumar Sethi, *The Business of Electronics: A Concise History*, Palgrave Macmillan, New York, 2013, p. 399.
AEG showcased the Magnetophon K1 at Berlin's 1935 Industrial Exhibition, but the world was not to discover the tape recorder until after the surrender of the Wehrmacht in 1945, when American soldiers stumbled across the machine and shipped a few of the devices to the U.S. for analysis.

7. Allgemeine Elektricitäts-Gesellschaft (AEG)
https://term.museum-digital.de/md-de/persinst/212911?lang=en
Accessed March 5, 2024.

8. Alison Owings, *Frauen: German Women Recall the Third Reich*, Rutgers University Press, New Bruswick, New Jersey, 1994, p. 37.
"We were actually all drafted into the BdM. [Almost] everyone in my class was in BdM. At the time, I didn't think about it. I thought, if the others do it and if it's so customary, one goes along, nicht?"

9. *Hitler Youth*, The History Place.
https://www.historyplace.com/worldwar2/hitleryouth/index.html
Accessed January 16, 2024.

10. Richard Bessel, *Life in the Third Reich*, Oxford University Press, Great Britain, 1987, p. XVI and XIX.

11. *Agfa Box Camera*. Lippisches Kamera Museum. http://www.lippisches-kameramuseum.de/Agfa/Agfa_Box_44.htm Accessed June 30, 2024.

By 1940, amateur photography was a well-developed hobby in Germany, made popular by the affordable price of the Agfa camera for only 4 Reichsmarks. However, as the war progressed, the photographic industry was commandeered to primarily equip propagandists.

12. Image is from Tilly's collection; unknown photographer.

13. Ibid.

14. Cynthia Sandor, (2016), *Bund Deutscher Mädel (Association of German Girls)*.
https://bdmhistory.com/1356/ Accessed June 26, 2024.

15. Earl Beck, *Under the Bombs*, The University Press of Kentucky, Lexington, 1986, p. 86.

16. Gesine Gerhard, *Nazi Hunger Politics: A History of Food in the Third Reich*, Rowman and Littlefield, New York, 2015, p. 40.

17. Ibid., p. 61-63.

18. Alice Weinreb, *Matters of Taste: The Politics of Food and Hunger in Divided Germany, 1945-1971*, Ph.D. Dissertation, University of Michigan, 2009, p. 47.

19. Malte Zierenberg, *Berlin's Black Market:1939-1950*, Palgrave Macmillan, London, 2015, p. 44.

20. Curt Riess, *The Berlin Story*, The Dial Press, New York, 1952, p. 4.

## Chapter 2: Among a Sea of Migrants

1. Earl Beck, *Under the Bombs*, The University Press of Kentucky, Lexington, 1986, p. 175.

2. Mary H. Williams, *U.S. Army in World War II Special Studies Chronology 1941-1945*, Office of the Chief of Military History, Washington, D.C., 1960, p. 496.

3. Leon Uris, *Armageddon*, Doubleday, New York, 1964, p. 63.

4. Earl Ziemke, *The U.S. Army in the Occupation of Germany 1944-1946*, Center of Military History, U.S. Army, Washington, D.C., 1975, p. 116.

5. Mary H. Williams, *U.S. Army in World War II Special Studies Chronology 1941-1945*, Office of the Chief of Military History, Washington, D.C., 1960, p. 496.

6. Ibid., p. 498.

7. Curt Riess, *The Berlin Story*, The Dial Press, New York, 1952, p. 31.

8. Mary H. Williams, *U.S. Army in World War II Special Studies Chronology 1941-1945*, Office of the Chief of Military History, Washington, D.C., 1960, p. 424.

9. Ibid., p. 510.

10. Ibid., p. 519.

## Chapter 3. Finding Relief in Freising

1. *Stadt Freising*, Gästemagazin der ältesten Stadt an der Isar, Rindermarkt 20. 85354 Freising, Germany.

2. Florian Notter, *Removal of Nazi Names and Insignia*, Fink das Magazin, Freising, Germany, June 2022. https://www.fink-magazin.de/removal-of-nazi-names-and-insignia/ Accessed August 8, 2024.

3. Anton Wandinger, *Freising von 1945 bis 1950*, Neue Munchner Verlags, Munich, Germany, 1950, p. 19.

4. Image is from Tilly's collection; unknown photographer.

5. Anton Wandinger, *Freising von 1945 bis 1950*, Neue Munchner Verlags, Munich, Germany, 1950, p. 86.

6. Earl Ziemke, *The U.S. Army in the Occupation of Germany 1944-1946*, Center of Military History, U.S. Army, Washington, D.C., 1975, p. 279.

The U.S. Army's immediate concerns were keeping routes of transport around Freising clear of homeless people clogging the roads, securing their shelter, care, and supervision, and returning them to their homes swiftly, if possible. The dangers of not adequately controlling the population included the threats of uprising or looting, but a greater menace was the potential for outbreaks of typhus, cholera, diphtheria, or dysentery.

7. Earl Ziemke, *The U.S. Army in the Occupation of Germany 1944-1946*, Center of Military History, U.S. Army, Washington, D.C., 1975, p. 331.

8. *Agricultural and Technological College at Weihenstephan*, Army Life and U.S. Army Recruiting News, Vol. 28, No. 7, July 1946. https://www.google.com/books/edition/Army_Life_and_U_S_Army_Recruiting_News/jDgwAAAAIAAJ?hl=en&gbpv=1&dq=weihenstephan+school,+US+forces+european+theater&pg=RA4-PA18&printsec=frontcover Accessed March 10, 2024.

9. Earl Ziemke, *The U.S. Army in the Occupation of Germany 1944-1946*, Center of Military History, U.S. Army, Washington, D.C., 1975, p. 330.

10. Anton Wandinger, *Freising von 1945 bis 1950*, Neue Munchner Verlags, Munich, Germany, 1950, p. 62.

11. Walter M. Hudson, *The U.S. Military Government and Democratic Reform and Denazification in Bavaria, 1945-47*, M. S. Thesis, U.S. Army Command and General Staff College, Ft. Leavenworth, Kansas, 2001, p. 120.

12. Ibid., p. 120

13. Anton Wandinger, *Freising von 1945 bis 1950*, Neue Munchner Verlags, Munich, Germany, 1950, p. 62.

14. Ibid., p. 78.

15. Earl Ziemke, *The U.S. Army in the Occupation of Germany 1944-1946*, Center of Military History, U.S. Army, Washington, D.C., 1975, p. 396.

16. John D. Hess, *Coping with Crisis: Military Government Officials, U.S. Policy, and the Occupation of Bavaria, 1945-1949*, Ph.D. Dissertation, University of Kansas, Lawrence, Kansas, 2017, p. 157.

17. Anton Wandinger, *Freising von 1945 bis 1950*, Neue Munchner Verlags, Munich, Germany, 1950, p. 74.

18. Earl Ziemke, *The U.S. Army in the Occupation of Germany 1944-1946*, Center of Military History, U.S. Army, Washington, D.C., 1975, p. 53.

19. Anton Wandinger, *Freising von 1945 bis 1950*, Neue Munchner Verlags, Munich, Germany, 1950, p. 55.

20. Dr. des. Isabella Hödl-Notter, IHN Geschichtsforschung, Marzling, Germany in a personal communication, October 12, 2025.
    The bridge across the Isar River in the photo was built out of wood by U.S. Army troops in 1945 as a temporary replacement after the original bridge was demolished by the retreating German army.

21. Joseph Rollins and Maria Rollins, *World War II Memories and Love Knows No Borders*, Trafford Publishing, Victoria, British Columbia, 2006, p. 137.

22. *Anton Schlüter*, https://de.wikipedia.org/wiki/Anton_Schlüter)_(Unternehmen) Accessed March 8, 2024.

23. Joseph Rollins and Maria Rollins, *World War II Memories and Love Knows No Borders*, Trafford Publishing, Victoria, British Columbia, 2006, p. 142.

24. Earl Ziemke, *The U.S. Army in the Occupation of Germany 1944-1946*, Center of Military History, U.S. Army, Washington, D.C., 1975, p. 411.

25. *The 1948 Annual Report of Freising Detachment, Germany, (Territory Under Allied Occupation, 1945-1955: U.S. Zone)*, Office of Military Government for Bavaria, Kreis Traunstein Records, Box 11, Field Operation Division, Area Offices Annual Historical Report, Freising, 1948. Hoover Institution Library and Archives, Stanford, California, p. 15.

In 1948, when asked by the Intelligence Division, OMG, about the progress of incorporating displaced civilians into Freising society, Captain Joseph F. Nordgren, commander of Stadtkreis Freising replied, "None." He expressed frustration with local officials for their "negligent attitude" toward finding a solution to the refugee problem, stating, "The assimilation of expellees into Bavarian social and religious life has not been accomplished because the Bavarians and expellees do not consider the present conditions permanent. And Bavarians consider the expellees as second class."

26. Image is from Tilly's collection; unknown photographer.

27. Ibid.

28. Harald Jähner, *Aftermath Life in the Fallout of the Third Reich, 1945-1955*, Alfred A. Knopf, New York, 2022, p. 244.

29. Ibid.

30. John Willoughby, *Remaking the Conquering Heroes: The Social and Geopolitical Impact of the Post War American Occupation of Germany*, Palgrave, New York, 2001, p. 32.

31. John Reese, Garmisch Recounts Day of the Tigers, U.S. Army, 2008. https://www.army.mil/article/10909/garmisch_recounts_day_of_the_tigers Accessed March 8, 2024.
Located high in the Alps, Garmisch and its neighbor, Partenkirchen, hosted the 1936 Winter Olympics. Visitors enjoyed taking gondola rides to a year-round hotel perched just below the Zugspitze, the highest peak in the Bavarian Alps. After the war, the town and surrounding areas became popular recreation sites for thousands of American soldiers stationed nearby, enriching local economies with military tourism.

32. Earl Ziemke, *The U.S. Army in the Occupation of Germany 1944-1946*, Center of Military History, U.S. Army, Washington, D.C., 1975, p. 332.

33. Image is from Tilly's collection; unknown photographer.

34. Ibid.

# Chapter 4. Embracing a Democratic Life

1. Anton Wandinger, *Freising von 1945 bis 1950*, Neue Munchner Verlags, Munich, Germany, 1950, p. 77.

2. John D. Hess, *Coping with Crisis: Military Government Officials, U.S. Policy, and the Occupation of Bavaria, 1945-1949*, Ph.D. Dissertation, University of Kansas, Lawrence, Kansas, 2017, p. 51.

3. Walter M. Hudson, *The U.S. Military Government and Democratic Reform and Denazification in Bavaria, 1945-47*, M. S. Thesis, U.S. Army Command and General Staff College, Ft. Leavenworth, Kansas, 2001, p. 80.

4. Earl Ziemke, *The U.S. Army in the Occupation of Germany 1944-1946*, Center of Military History, U.S. Army, Washington, D.C., 1975, p. 401.

5. Ibid., p. 402-403.

6. Military Government Weekly Bulletin No. 15, November 1945, Office of Military Government, U.S. Forces European Theater, University of Wisconsin at Madison. https://search.library.wisc.edu/digital/ARZZW7UXGKLTZZ8J/pages?as=text&view=scroll Accessed March 10, 2024, p. 30-35.

7. Walter M. Hudson, *The U.S. Military Government and Democratic Reform and Denazification in Bavaria, 1945-47*, M. S. Thesis, U.S. Army Command and General Staff College, Ft. Leavenworth, Kansas, 2001, p. 17.

8. Earl Ziemke, *The U.S. Army in the Occupation of Germany 1944-1946*, Center of Military History, U.S. Army, Washington, D.C., 1975, p.70.

9. Ibid., p. 360.

10. John D. Hess, *Coping with Crisis: Military Government Officials, U.S. Policy, and the Occupation of Bavaria, 1945-1949*, Ph.D. Dissertation, University of Kansas, Lawrence, Kansas, 2017, p. 225–226.

11. Earl Ziemke, *The U.S. Army in the Occupation of Germany 1944-1946*, Center of Military History, U.S. Army, Washington, D.C., 1975, p. 141.

12. Walter M. Hudson, *The U.S. Military Government and Democratic Reform and Denazification in Bavaria, 1945-47*, M. S. Thesis, U.S. Army Command and General Staff College, Ft. Leavenworth, Kansas, 2001, p. 176.

13. Earl Ziemke, *The U.S. Army in the Occupation of Germany 1944-1946*, Center of Military History, U.S. Army, Washington, D.C., 1975, p. 429.

14. Ibid., p. 372.

15. *Amerikahaus*-Munich. https://www.amerikahaus.de/en/about-us/history Accessed April 5, 2024.
The U.S. Government's Reorientation Program to encourage democratization, while well-established in Munich, was limited in Freising to periodic films. According to the military government commander, Captain Joseph F. Nordgren, Freising's film program needed to improve. "In order to interest the children as well as attract the adults, each program should consist of a newsreel, a cultural film, and a short entertainment film instead of showing only cultural films which the children do not understand and are of little interest to most adults."

16. Ibid.

17. John D. Hess, *Coping with Crisis: Military Government Officials, U.S. Policy, and the Occupation of Bavaria, 1945-1949*, Ph.D. Dissertation, University of Kansas, Lawrence, Kansas, 2017, p. 251–254.

18. Walter M. Hudson, *The U.S. Military Government and Democratic Reform and Denazification in Bavaria, 1945-47*, M. S. Thesis, U.S. Army Command and General Staff College, Ft. Leavenworth, Kansas, 2001, p. 27.

19. Ibid., p. 48-50.

20. *The 1948 Annual Report of Area Freising, Germany, (Territory Under Allied Occupation, 1945-1955: U.S. Zone)*, Office of Military Government for Bavaria, Kreis Traunstein Records, Box 11, Field Operation Division, Area Offices Annual Historical Report, Freising, 1948, Hoover Institution Library and Archives, Stanford, California, p. 19.

21. Ibid., p. 7.

22. Guido Hoyer, *Freising im 20. Jahrhundert (1918-1992), in: Stadtarchiv Freising (Hg.): Freising.* Eine Stadtgeschichte Erscheinungstermin Frühjahr, 2026, p. 112.

23. *The 1948 Annual Report of Area Freising, Germany, (Territory Under Allied Occupation, 1945-1955: U.S. Zone)*, Office of Military Government for Bavaria, Kreis Traunstein Records, Box 11, Field Operation Division, Area Offices Annual Historical Report, Freising, 1948, Hoover Institution Library and Archives, Stanford, California, p. 15 and p. 19.

24. John D. Hess, *Coping with Crisis: Military Government Officials, U.S. Policy, and the Occupation of Bavaria, 1945-1949*, Ph.D. Dissertation, University of Kansas, Lawrence, Kansas, 2017, p. 341.

25. Earl Ziemke, *The U.S. Army in the Occupation of Germany 1944-1946*, Center of Military History, U.S. Army, Washington, D.C., 1975, p. 274.

26. John D. Hess, *Coping with Crisis: Military Government Officials, U.S. Policy, and the Occupation of Bavaria, 1945-1949*, Ph.D. Dissertation, University of Kansas, Lawrence, Kansas, 2017, p. 88.

27. Ibid., p. 103.

28. *The 1948 Annual Report of Area Freising, Germany, (Territory Under Allied Occupation, 1945-1955: U.S. Zone)*, Office of Military Government for Bavaria, Kreis Traunstein Records, Box 11, Field Operation Division, Area Offices Annual Historical Report, Freising, 1948, Hoover Institution Library and Archives, Stanford, California, p. 83.

29. Military Government Weekly Bulletin No. 5, August 1945, Office of Military Government, U.S. Forces European Theater, University of Wisconsin at Madison, p. 3-7. https://search.library.wisc.edu/digital/A2UVRZLV74S3ZZ84/pages/ALV5WN5PJCPFWB9C Accessed March 10, 2024

30. John D. Hess, *Coping with Crisis: Military Government Officials, U.S. Policy, and the Occupation of Bavaria, 1945-1949*, Ph.D. Dissertation, University of Kansas, Lawrence, Kansas, 2017, p. 98.

31. Ibid., p. 305.

# Chapter 5. New Friendships

1. Shannon L. Fogg, *Stealing Home: Looting, Restitution, and Reconstructing Jewish Lives in France, 1942–1947*, Oxford University press, United Kingdom, 2017, p. 126.

The Hauge Convention is a series of treaties and declarations, begun in 1899, that addresses the conduct of warfare. The right of requisition as recognized by the Hauge Convention allows only the supplies and objects that are needed for the maintenance of the army in the territory they occupy and does not include the large-scale transport of supplies to benefit the home industry of the invading army. The spoiling of supplies and property is outlawed.

2. Anton Wandinger, *Freising von 1945 bis 1950*, Neue Munchner Verlags, Munich, Germany, 1950, p. 63–64.

3. Image is from Tilly's collection; unknown photographer.

4. Ibid.

5. Andreas Beschorner, *201 Jahre Garrisonsstadt Freising*, Fink das Magazin, Freising, Germany, March 2010.
http://www.supershit.com/vonhier/img/finkmagazin/pdf/33.pdf
Accessed November 3, 2024.

6. Source: Britta von Rettberg, Author: USAAF, (1945, April 25), *Post attack (April 18, 1945) aerial picture of Freising.*
https://commons.wikimedia.org/wiki/File:Freising_(USAAF_1945-04-25).png Accessed November 5, 2024.

7. *Transcript of Monthly Reports, 1946-1950, 604th Tactical Control Squadron, U.S. Army, 501st Tactical C Group, XII Tactical Air Command,* Source: Air Force Historical Research Agency, U.S. Air Force, Maxwell Air Force Base, Alabama, p. 1046.

8. *Air Force Lineage and Honors: 604th Aircraft Control and Warning Squadron*, (2012, March 10), Air Force Historical Research Agency, U.S. Air Force, Maxwell Air Force Base, Alabama.
http://ww.35.usafunithistory.com/PDF/0600/604%20AIRCRAFT%20CONTROL%20AND%20WARNING%20SQ.pdf
Accessed February 2, 2024.

9. Patricia Parrish, *Forty-five Years of Vigilance for Freedom: U.S. Air Forces in Europe, 1942-1987*, Office of History, Headquarters, U.S. Air Forces in Europe, Ramstein Air Base, Germany, 1987, p. 21.

10. Walter Elkins, *US Air Forces in Europe Units and Kasernes, 1945-1989.*
https://www.usarmygermany.com/Sont.htm?https&&&www.usarmygermany.com/USAFE%20TACS.htm Accessed February 1, 2024.

11. *Transcript of Monthly Reports, 1946-1950, 604th Tactical Control Squadron, U.S. Army, 501st Tactical C Group, XII Tactical Air Command,* Source: Air Force Historical Research Agency, U.S. Air Force, Maxwell Air Force Base, Alabama, p. 760.

12. Randall Degering, *Radar Contact: The Beginnings of Army Air Forces Radar and Fighter Control*, Air University Press, Maxwell Air Force Base, Alabama, 2018, p. 79.

13. Ibid., p. 79.

14. Ibid., p. 80.

15. *Transcript of Monthly Reports, 1946-1950, 604th Tactical Control Squadron, U.S. Army, 501st Tactical C Group, XII Tactical Air Command,* Source: Air Force Historical Research Agency, U.S. Air Force, Maxwell Air Force Base, Alabama, p. 1047.

16. Randall Degering, *Radar Contact: The Beginnings of Army Air Forces Radar and Fighter Control*, Air University Press, Maxwell Air Force Base, Alabama, 2018, p. 82.

17. *Transcript of Monthly Reports, 1946-1950, 604th Tactical Control Squadron, U.S. Army, 501st Tactical C Group, XII Tactical Air Command,* Source: Air Force Historical Research Agency, U.S. Air Force, Maxwell Air Force Base, Alabama, p. 527.

18. Ibid., p. 510.

19. Image is from Tilly's collection; unknown photographer.

20. *Transcript of Monthly Reports, 1946-1950, 604th Tactical Control Squadron, U.S. Army, 501st Tactical C Group, XII Tactical Air Command,* Source: Air Force Historical Research Agency, U.S. Air Force, Maxwell Air Force Base, Alabama, p. 495.

21. Kali Martin, *Sending Hope to Europe: The First Care Packages Arrive in 1946*, The National World War II Museum, New Orleans, Louisiana, May 10, 2021. https://www.nationalww2museum.org/war/articles/sending-hope-europe-first-care-packages-arrive-1946 Accessed October 15, 2024.

22. John D. Hess, *Coping with Crisis: Military Government Officials, U.S. Policy, and the Occupation of Bavaria, 1945-1949*, Ph.D. Dissertation, University of Kansas, Lawrence, Kansas, 2017, p. 155.

23. Monica Wang, *From Enemy to Family: German War Brides and U.S.-German Rapprochement, 1945-1950,* Yale University, 2018, p. 35.

24. David F. Winkler, (1997), *Searching the Skies: The Legacy of the United States Cold War Defense Radar Program*, U.S. Air Force Headquarters Air Combat Command, Langley Air Force Base, Virginia. https://nuke.fas.org/guide/usa/airdef/1997-06-01955.pdf Accessed September 20, 2024, p. 15.

25. John D. Hess, *Coping with Crisis: Military Government Officials, U.S. Policy, and the Occupation of Bavaria, 1945-1949*, Ph.D. Dissertation, University of Kansas, Lawrence, Kansas, 2017, p. 340.

26. The National Security Act of 1947. Air Force Historical Support Division. https://www.afhistory.af.mil/FAQs/Fact-Sheets/Article/458989/1947-the-national-security-act-of-1947/ Accessed September 20, 2024

## Chapter 6. Charting a Different Path

1. *Transcript of Monthly Reports, 1946-1950, 604th Tactical Control Squadron, U.S. Army, 501st Tactical C Group, XII Tactical Air Command,* Source: Air Force Historical Research Agency, U.S. Air Force, Maxwell Air Force Base, Alabama, p. 536.

2. Ibid., p. 541.

3. Ibid., p. 579.

4. *Transcript of Monthly Reports, 1946-1950, 604th Tactical Control Squadron, U.S. Army, 501st Tactical C Group, XII Tactical Air Command,* Source: Air Force Historical Research Agency, U.S. Air Force, Maxwell Air Force Base, Alabama, p. 521.

In spring 1946, the U.S. Armed Forces found their answer to this potential problem by introducing the German Youth Activities (GYA) program. The 604th Tactical Control Squadron took charge of the GYA program in Freising in June, 1946. Since the 1930s, young Germans had absorbed American entertainment to lift their spirits with music and Hollywood stars—even Walt Disney's Mickey Mouse was popular. By August 1948, there were 945 children enrolled in the Freising district's GYA program.

5. Edward B. James, *The U.S. Forces German Youth Activities Program, 1945–1955*, Historical Division, Headquarters, U.S. Army Europe, 1956, p. 5.
https://ia804604.us.archive.org/12/items/HitlerYouth/US%20Armed%20Forces%20German%20Youth%20Activities%20Programs.pdf
Accessed July 24, 2025.

6. Petra Goedde, *GIs and Germans—Culture, Gender and Foreign Relations, 1945-1949*, Yale University Press, New Haven, Connecticut, 2003, p. 148.

7. Randall Degering, *Radar Contact: The Beginnings of Army Air Forces Radar and Fighter Control*, Air University Press, Maxwell Air Force Base, Alabama, 2018, p. 76.

8. Image is from Tilly's collection; unknown photographer.

9. Ibid.

10. *Transcript of Monthly Reports, 1946-1950, 604th Tactical Control Squadron, U.S. Army, 501st Tactical C Group, XII Tactical Air Command,* Source: Air Force Historical Research Agency, U.S. Air Force, Maxwell Air Force Base, Alabama, p. 560.

11. John D. Hess, *Coping with Crisis: Military Government Officials, U.S. Policy, and the Occupation of Bavaria, 1945-1949*, Ph.D. Dissertation, University of Kansas, Lawrence, Kansas, 2017, p. 183.

12. Ibid., p. 135.

While food shortages in Bavaria remained, the situation was better than expected. Dampening the enthusiasm of the Bavarians were the edicts from the Bizonal Economic Council, which required them to ship a good share of their harvest to the north. Established in June 1947, the Bizonal Economic Council aimed to improve economic reconstruction, especially food production and distribution, in an area called Bizonia, created by merging the British and American occupation zones on January 1, 1947.

13. *The 1948 Annual Report of Area Freising, Germany, (Territory Under Allied Occupation, 1945-1955: U.S. Zone),* Office of Military Government for Bavaria, Kreis Traunstein Records, Box 11, Field Operation Division, Area Offices Annual Historical Report, Freising, 1948, Hoover Institution Library and Archives, Stanford, California, p. 27.

The Bizonal Economic Council's decrees were disliked because "The farmers feel that Bizonia is unfair to them. The Bavarians are forced to send food to northern Germany's industrialized Ruhr Valley; however, the industrialized north is not forced to reciprocate by sending farm equipment to Bavaria." In particular, the cattle collection program, where Bavarian farmers had to surrender their cattle to meet production quotas, "was decidedly unpopular." The people blamed the Bizonal Economic Council and the military government for sponsoring such a loathsome program.

14. Anton Wandinger, *Freising von 1945 bis 1950*, Neue Munchner Verlags, Munich, Germany, 1950, p. 86.

15. *Robert G. Moeller, Protecting Motherhood*: Women and the Family in the Politics of Post- war Germany, University of California Press, Berkeley, California, 1993, p. 2.

16. Walter Elkins, *US Air Forces in Europe Units and Kasernes, 1945-1989.* https://www.usarmygermany.com/Sont.htm?https&&&www.usarmygermany.com/USAFE%20TACS.htm Accessed February 1, 2024.

17. John D. Hess, *Coping with Crisis: Military Government Officials, U.S. Policy, and the Occupation of Bavaria, 1945-1949*, Ph.D. Dissertation, University of Kansas, Lawrence, Kansas, 2017, p. 191.

However, the pent-up demand for consumer goods unleashed by currency reform outpaced supply. With high demand, prices soared. The people of Freising became distressed about the high prices. Until the demand for consumer goods was met, prices remained high.

18. Roger G. Miller, *To Save a City: The Berlin Airlift 1948-49*, Air Force History and Museums Program, 1998, p. 21. https://archive.org/details/ToSaveACityBerlinAirlift Accessed December 3, 2024.

19. Carroll V. Glines, (2006, June 12), *Operation Vittles: The Allied Airlift that Saved Berlin*, History Net. https://www.historynet.com/berlin-airlift-operation-vittles/ Accessed December 3, 2024.

20. *1949-The Berlin Airlift*, Air Force Historical Support Division. https://www.afhistory.af.mil/FAQs/Fact-Sheets/Article/458961/1949-the-berlin-airlift/ Accessed December 3, 2024.

21. Carroll V. Glines, (2006, June 12), *Operation Vittles: The Allied Airlift that Saved Berlin*, History Net. https://www.historynet.com/berlin-airlift-operation-vittles/ Accessed December 3, 2024.

22. *Transcript of Monthly Reports, 1946-1950, 604th Tactical Control Squadron, U.S. Army, 501st Tactical C Group, XII Tactical Air Command,* Source: Air Force Historical Research Agency, U.S. Air Force, Maxwell Air Force Base, Alabama, p. 681.

23. *60th Troop Carrier Wing*, Army Air Corps Museum and Library, Irving, Texas.
https://www.armyaircorpsmuseum.org/60th_Troop_Carrier_Wing.cfm Accessed December 2, 2024.

24. *Douglas C-47 Skytrain*, National Museum of the U.S. Air Force, Wright-Patterson Air Force Base, Dayton, Ohio.
https://www.nationalmuseum.af.mil/Visit/Museum-Exhibits/Fact-Sheets/Display/Article/196271/douglas-c-47d-skytrain/
Accessed December 2, 2024.

Eastham had a copilot and a radio operator on runs in the "Gooney Bird," an affectionate nickname for the C-47 derived from a character in the Popeye comic strip. His ship was modified for military transport with powerful twin Pratt and Whitney engines, large cargo doors, and a reinforced floor for heavy loads. With a maximum speed of 232 mph, a service ceiling of 26,400 feet, and a range of 1,500 miles, it could carry up to 3 tons.

25. James D. Eastham, (2016), *Obituary*, Robert Barham Funeral Home, Meridian, Mississippi.
https://www.robertbarhamffh.com/obituary/6364392
Accessed October 30, 2024.

26. *1949-The Berlin Airlift*, Air Force Historical Support Division.
https://www.afhistory.af.mil/FAQs/Fact-Sheets/Article/458961/1949-the-berlin-airlift/
Accessed December 3, 2024.

27. *Bulletin of the Combined Airlift Task Force*, Vol. 1, No. 11, September 7, 1948, The Allied Museum, Berlin. https://www.airlift-berlin.com/newspaper-task-force-times.html
Accessed December 5, 2024.

A newsletter just for the airlift men, *The Task Force Times*, printed a daily tally of achievements to spur competition among crews. On September 6, 1948, it noted that pilots with the 60th Troop Carrier Group made seventy-nine runs to Berlin in their C-47s, hauling 261 tons of supplies that day.

28. Stewart M. Powell, *The Berlin Airlift*, Air and Space Forces Magazine, Arlington, Virginia, 1998, June 1.
https://www.airandspaceforces.com/article/0698berlin/
Accessed December 5, 2024.

29. Kali Martin, *Sending Hope to Europe: The First Care Packages Arrive in 1946*, The National World War II Museum, New Orleans, Louisiana, 2021.
https://www.nationalww2museum.org/war/articles/sending-hope-europe-first-care-packages-arrive-1946 Accessed October 15, 2024.

30. Roger G. Miller, *To Save a City: The Berlin Airlift 1948-49*, Air Force History and Museums Program, 1998, p. 56.
https://archive.org/details/ToSaveACityBerlinAirlift
Accessed December 3, 2024.

31. *Transcript of Monthly Reports, 1946-1950, 604th Tactical Control Squadron, U.S. Army, 501st Tactical C Group, XII Tactical Air Command,* Source: Air Force Historical Research Agency, U.S. Air Force, Maxwell Air Force Base, Alabama, p. 785.

32. Ibid., p. 750.

33. Carroll V. Glines, (2006, June 12), *Operation Vittles: The Allied Airlift that Saved Berlin*, History Net.
https://www.historynet.com/berlin-airlift-operation-vittles/
Accessed December 3, 2024.

When the Soviets realized the airlift was working, they unleashed frustration through increased harassment of the unarmed cargo planes. Soviet fighters buzzed and dived the cargo planes, fired flak and rockets, and dropped strings of bombs, narrowly missing the aircraft. Once, a Soviet pilot came too close and crashed into a British plane, killing everyone. The Soviets positioned an anti-aircraft artillery unit to fire incendiary bullets between planes as they approached Gatow. They released barrage balloons dangling steel cables to float directly into the flight paths of cargo planes, creating severe collision risks. They jammed radio frequencies, shot flares, and aimed searchlights into cockpits to temporarily blind the airlift pilots. American and British airmen logged over seven hundred incidents of Soviet harassment.

34. Roger G. Miller, *To Save a City: The Berlin Airlift 1948-49*, Air Force History and Museums Program, 1998, p. 17.
https://archive.org/details/ToSaveACityBerlinAirlift
Accessed December 3, 2024

    The USAF had only a few tactical air fighter assets left in West Germany, an inadequate force to confront Soviet intimidation. To deter the Soviets from provoking an aerial war, LeMay ordered Lockheed F-80 Shooting Star jet fighters to Fürstenfeldbruck Air Base from the Panama Canal Zone. The single-seat jet was powered by an Allison turbojet engine with a maximum speed of 580 mph, a service ceiling of 46,800 feet, and a range of 1,090 miles. The pilot had Browning machine guns, high-velocity air-to-ground rockets, and two 1,000-pound bombs at his disposal. Assigned to pilot the F-80, Eastham had to adapt to the sensation created by speeds approaching Mach 1. His job at Fürstenfeldbruck through 1949 included air defense, photo-reconnaissance, and patrolling West Germany's border with Soviet-occupied East Germany. Additional American fighter aircraft safeguarding West Germany ensured that the Soviets seriously considered the consequences of escalating harassment tactics.

35. *Transcript of Monthly Reports, 1946-1950, 604th Tactical Control Squadron, U.S. Army, 501st Tactical C Group, XII Tactical Air Command,* Source: Air Force Historical Research Agency, U.S. Air Force, Maxwell Air Force Base, Alabama, p. 842.

36. Ibid., p. 855.

37. Roger G. Miller, *To Save a City: The Berlin Airlift 1948-49*, Air Force History and Museums Program, 1998, p. 105.
https://archive.org/details/ToSaveACityBerlinAirlift
Accessed December 3, 2024.

Flights continued through September to build a reserve in case the Soviets reimposed the blockade. Accidents dimmed the glory of the airlift and left a sober reminder of the sacrifices given by thirty-nine British, thirty-one American, and thirteen German men who lost their lives from plane crashes and ground incidents.

38. Ibid., p. 28.

39. Image is from Tilly's collection; unknown photographer.

# English Meaning of German Words

*Arbeitslager.* Labor camp.

*Arbeitsmädel.* Work maiden. The National Labor Program, Reichsarbeitdienst (RAD), required able-bodied high school graduates to serve the Third Reich for six months. An unmarried young woman working in the women's RAD section was referred to as an *Arbeitsmädel.*

*Auf Wiedersehen.* Good bye.

*Berliner Luftbrücke.* The Berlin Airlift. The Allied monumental air mission to deliver food and fuel aid to West Berlin during the Soviet blockade of land and water routes lasted from June 24, 1948, to September 30, 1949. The airlift carried 2,325,510 tons of cargo, with coal comprising most of the load, followed by food and miscellaneous goods.

*Der Hungerwinter.* The Hunger Winter of 1946–1947. Malnutrition hovered over postwar Europe during one of the coldest winters on record when food and heating fuel were scarce.

*Der Kleine Muck.* A German fairy tale about a misshapen little boy who lives in the Near East named Little Muck. He becomes orphaned, sets out on a journey across the desert, attains magic powers, and finds a hidden treasure, but unfortunately is mistreated by others. Despite facing many challenges, Little Muck grows wise through his experiences. The story's moral is that people should not be judged by their appearance; instead, Little Muck deserves admiration rather than mockery.

*Eintopf.* A spartan stew cooked in one pot and made with varied foods, such as potatoes, cabbage, carrots, sausage, etc. During World War II, Nazi propagandists encouraged German housewives to prepare one-pot meals with inexpensive vegetables and cuts of meat because food and cooking fuel were scarce. The Nazis promoted the *Eintopf* as a sacrifice to strengthen the war effort.

*Ersatz or E-Kaserne.* Replacement barracks. The E-Kaserne was one of three barracks built or expanded by the Wehrmacht in Freising during the 1930s. After the war, the U.S. Army Air Corps, 604th Tactical Control Squadron, took possession of the E-Kaserne and reconditioned the barracks into a base.

*Flakhelfer.* German youth drafted to assist the Luftwaffe in operating anti-aircraft guns. They also acted as lookouts, radar operators, and in communications.

*Fragebogen.* A lengthy and comprehensive questionnaire devised by the Allies to denazify German society of Nazi ideology by identifying and arresting Nazi Party members and barring them from employment in positions of influence with the U.S. Army or in German private and public sectors.

*Führer.* Leader. A term often used when referring to Adolph Hitler.

*Hausmeister.* Building supervisor, caretaker, or maintenance person. The U.S. Army hired Richard and Ilse Pirkl to take care of the requisitioned buildings on Ganzenmüllerstraße housing the bachelor officers of the 604th Tactical Control Squadron and their civilian German housekeepers.

*Kreisspruchkammern.* City investigative tribunal. In 1946, the Allies turned the responsibility of denazification over to the Germans, who established civilian tribunals to judge the accused for their involvement with the Nazi Party.

*Landkreis.* Rural district or county.

*Landrat.* Administrator or chief administrative officer of a Landkreis or district.

*Lebensraum.* Living space for Germans. The quest for more room or land for the German people was a political priority of Adolph Hitler and a critical component of the Nazi ideology that drove their policies. In the 1930s, German domestic food production did not meet the needs of the people, thus forcing them to rely on imported food. Reliance on imports left the population vulnerable to blockades and tariffs, which, during World War I, caused the starvation deaths of thousands of Germans. Hitler's solution to achieving nutritional self-sufficiency was territorial expansion by conquest.

*Mädels*: Young women.

*Oberbürgermeister.* Lord mayor or head of government of a Stadtkreis or city.

*Putzfrau.* Charwoman, cleaning woman.

*Rathaus.* City Hall.

*Regierungsbezirk.* A governmental district or administrative region in some German federal states. It is an intermediate level of administration that is responsible for governmental decisions affecting smaller districts within its jurisdiction. The U.S. Military Government adopted the *Regierungsbezirk* designation for its regional oversight of field detachments. For example, field detachments in the *Regierungsbezirk* of Oberbayern were supervised by the military government headquartered in Munich.

*Stadtkreis.* City or urban district.

*Trümmerfrauen.* Women who cleared rubble and scavenged bricks from bombed buildings after World War II. The Allies employed women or hired private contractors to use women for demolishing unsafe buildings and saving debris for reconstruction. The women received a small wage and were issued one daily food ration card.

*Volksdeutsche.* Ethnic Germans living outside of Germany who were not German citizens. A significant portion of Volksdeutsche lived in Eastern European countries that belonged to Germany before World War I. After the defeat of Nazi Germany, many Volksdeutsche were considered traitors in their adopted countries and were forcibly expelled from their homes into mainly southern Germany.

*Volksgemeinschaft.* Life of the German national community. The concept emphasized a unified national identity and purpose. The Nazi party reinterpreted this concept to rally German support for the war. National socialist planners formulated a rationing system to manage scarce food supplies, urging people to subordinate their interests to the collective good. While promising that everyone in the national community would be treated equally, in reality, those considered inferior were deprived of privileges.

*Weltanschauung.* Worldview. The Nazi *Weltanschauung* included beliefs in Aryan supremacy, antisemitism, patriarchy, nationalism, expansionism, and an authoritarian state.

# Index

## A
aircraft
    Avro Lancaster, xvi
    B-17 Flying Fortress, xvi, xvii, 88, 96, 109
    B-24 Liberator, xvi, xvii, 109
    Douglas C-47 Skytrain (Gooney Bird), 95, 96, 130
    Douglas C-54 Skymaster, 95, 98
    Lockheed F-80 Shooting Star, 101, 132
    Messerschmitt Bf 109, 21, 111
    Messerschmitt Bf 110, 111
    P-38 Lightning, xvi, 110
    P-47 Thunderbolt, xvi, 86, 88, 89, 110
    P-51 Mustang, xvi, xvii, 86, 88, 89, 110
Allgemeine Elektricitäts Gesellschaft (AEG), 1–3, 5, 9, 10, 12, 14, 15, 27, 112, 113
    electron microscope, 2, 113
    Fritz Pfleumer, 2
    Magnetophon K1, tape recorder, 2, 113
Allies, Allied Forces, ix–xi, xv, xvi, 3, 7, 9, 14, 15, 17, 19, 20, 22, 23, 26, 30, 45, 57, 61, 70, 83, 94, 104, 108, 109, 111, 118, 122, 123, 128–131, 135–138, 152
Amerikahaus in Munich, 50, 121
American Express Company, 105
anti-aircraft guns, xvii, 4, 109, 111, 136
antisemitism, 53, 138

## B
Bad Kissingen, 80
Baden-Württemberg, 46
Baltic Sea, states, 7, 58
Bavaria, Bavarian, vii, xiv, 16, 17, 20, 22, 23, 29, 33, 36, 39–41, 46, 50, 52, 56, 59, 76, 79, 117–123, 126, 128, 129
Bayreuth, 20

Berlin
  airlift, *Berliner Luftbrücke*, Operation Vittles, xi, 94–96, 98, 99, 101, 103, 129–133
  Berlin Air Offensive, 108
  February 3, 1945, Mission 817, xv–xvii, 1, 9, 11, 107, 109, 111, 112
  Gatow Airport, British sector, 131
  Industrial Exhibition, 1935, 113
  Soviet blockade of, xi, 98, 132, 133, 135
  Tempelhof Airport, American sector, 96, 97
  Tempelhof marshalling yard, railyard, xvii, xviii, 109
  West Berlin, 94–96, 98, 101, 103, 135
Bizonia, Bizonal Economic Council, 128
black market, xi, 9, 21, 47, 53, 55, 57, 77, 114
bombs
  explosive, xvi, xviii, 20
  incendiary, xvi, 20
Bremen enclave, 46
Bremerhaven, port of, 43
*Bund deutscher Mädel*, 3, 114

# C

cameras
  Agfa Box 44, xii, 5, 36, 114
  Kodak 35 Rangefinder, 36
  Rolleicord, xii, 66
Catholic church, 46, 52
Christian Social Union political party, 52
Christmas holiday, events, 35, 76, 89, 100, 101
Clay, Lucius D., Gen., 45, 52, 57, 59, 94, 107
Club, 20 MPH, at the 604th TCS, 86–88, 96
coal, fuel shortage, 9, 29, 30, 50, 79, 95, 97, 103, 135
Cold War, 81, 126
Communist political party, rule, bloc, 19, 52, 59, 80, 83, 90, 94, 95, 100
Cooperative for American Remittances to Europe (CARE), 76, 78, 79, 97, 126, 13
curfew, 15, 30, 31
Czechoslovakia, 14, 58, 59, 90

## D

D-Day, 108
Dachau, 28
Darmstadt, 80
DDT powder, 30, 47
demagogues, 53, 56, 152
democracy, democratization, viii–xii, 45, 47–50, 52, 54, 62, 83, 85, 104, 107, 117, 120, 121, 151, 152
demobilization, 42
denazification, 27, 32, 48, 49, 117, 120, 121, 137, 151
*Der Kleine Muck,* 89, 135
diseases
    cholera, 116
    diphtheria, 116
    dysentery, 116
    typhus, 30, 116
    tuberculosis, 44
dislocated civilians, 24, 28, 30, 36, 45, 53, 56, 90, 151
Distinguished Flying Cross, 69, 89
Doolittle, James H., Lt. Gen., xv, xvi, 108–112

## E

East Anglia, England, xv–xvii
Eastern Europe, 22, 80, 90, 138
Eisenhower, Dwight D., Gen., 26, 39
emigrate, 77, 98
Erzgebirge Mountains, 14, 17
evacuee, 13, 24
expellee, ix, 58, 118 (see also *Volksdeutsche*)

## F

Federal Republic of Germany, 104
*Flakhelfer,* 111, 136
flak, towers, xvii, 4, 88, 108, 110, 111, 131
food insecurity
    *der Hungerwinter 1946-1947,* 75, 135
    *Eintopf,* 8, 136
    hunger, x, xi, 3, 5, 8, 16, 19, 22, 35, 54, 75, 79, 98, 114, 152

imports, 57, 137
production and distribution problems, xi, 5, 54, 57, 128, 137
rations, 8, 9, 35, 55, 57, 86
*Fragebogen,* 28, 136
France, 15, 108
Frauenkirche in Munich, 50, 51
Freising
    Fischergasse prison, 28, 31
    Ganzenmüllerstraße, 61–65, 69, 87, 136
    Ganzenmüllerstraße women
        Berta, 64, 67, 87
        Fanni, 64
        Gusti, 64
        Hilda, 64
        Jonni, 64
    *Landkreis* (district), 52, 56, 137
    *Landrat,* 52, 137
    Marienplatz, 24, 25
    Obere Hauptstraße, 44
    orphans, 89, 101
    residents
        Pirkl, Richard and Ilse, *Hausmeister,* 64, 65, 136
        Schlüter, Anton, 34, 118
    St. George's Parish Church, 24, 25
    St. Mary and St. Corbinian Cathedral, 23, 24
    Schlüterhof estate, 27, 33, 34, 37, 63, 65, 76
    Schlüterhof women
        Gertrud, 35, 37
        Kläre, 35, 37
        Lilo, 35, 37
        Maria, 35, 37
        Martha, 35, 37
        Rosi, 35
        Schumacher, Gertrud, 37–39, 41, 43
    *Stadtkreis* (city), 43, 52, 118, 137, 138
    Weihenstephan Benedictine monastery, 23, 33
Fulda, 97
Fürstenfeldbruck Air Force Base, 101, 132

## G

Garmisch/Partenkirchen, 39–42, 119
German cultural rehabilitation, reorientation, 39, 121
German economic recovery, 49, 90
German Youth Activities (GYA), 85, 86, 127
Great Britian's Royal Air Force (RAF), xvi, 107, 108
Greater Hessen, 46
ground-controlled approach operator (GCA), 97

## H

Halvorson, Gail S., Lt., 98
Hamburg, port of, 105
Harris, Arthur T., Sir, xv, 108, 109
Hof, 16, 17, 20
housing shortage, 17, 29, 45, 56, 62, 108
Hungary, 58, 59

## I

indigenous civilian employee, 55, 58, 83, 90
International Red Cross, 58
Isar River, 23, 24, 31, 32, 117

## J

Jews, 28, 53, 56, 78

## K

*Kasernes*
    E Kaserne, *Ersatz Kaserne,* 67, 68, 136
    General von Stein Kaserne, 68
    Vimy Kaserne, 68
*Kreispruchkammern,* 49, 137

## L

Lager Giesebitz, Pomerania, 5
Lager Hohenzollerndorf, Pomerania, 5, 6

LeMay, Curtis E., Gen., 81, 94, 95, 132

# M
Magdeburg, xvii
Mänk, Wachau Valley, Austria, 12
Marshall, George C., Gen., 26
money/economics
    Deutschmark, 94
    Marshall Plan, 90
    Reichsmark, 7, 31, 76, 94, 114
Munich, viii, 16, 20, 22, 50, 51, 56, 76, 98, 121, 138

# N
Nationalsozialistische Deutsche Arbeiterpartei
    6th Panzer Army, 109
    Gestapo, xvi, xviii
    Goebbels, Joseph, 3
    Himmler, Heinrich, 3
    Hitler, Adolph, *Führer,* xi, xv, xviii, 2–4, 8, 11, 32, 61, 108, 136, 137
    Hitler Youth, 3, 4, 28, 113
    *Lebensraum*, 8, 137
    Luftwaffe, xvi, 109, 110, 111, 136
    Nazi, vii–xii, xv–xvii, 2–4, 6–9, 14, 16–21, 23, 27, 28, 32, 45, 47–49, 52–54, 56, 57, 85, 92, 94, 108–115, 136–138, 151, 152
    patriarchal mission, 2, 138, 151
    Reichsarbeitdienst (RAD) *Arbeitsmädel*, 5–7, 35, 135
        Edith, 5, 6
        Elsbet, 5, 6
        Hanne, 6
        Hannelore, 5, 6
        Hilde, 5, 6
        Ilse, 5
        Lia, 5, 6
        Lotte, 5, 6
        Marianne, 5, 6
    Schutzstaffel (SS), 3
    War Economy Regulation, 9

Wehrmacht, 11, 16, 20, 67, 111, 113, 136
*Weltanschauung,* 2, 138
Neustadt, 80
New York, 43, 106
Nonfraternization, 39
Nuremberg, 20

## O

*Oberbürgermeister,* 52, 137
occupation zones, 15, 16, 19, 26, 39, 45, 46, 54, 57, 59, 70, 71, 75, 90, 94, 97, 104, 128
Offices of the Military Government, United States (OMGUS), 19, 45, 46, 48–50

## P

Peenemunde, 12
    Kühl, Helga, 12
    V-2 rocket, 4
    von Braun, Wernher, 12
photography, x, xii, 36, 37, 66, 91, 114, 153
Poland, Polish, xvi, 7, 15, 18, 58, 59
Prussia, 15
*Putzfrau,* 61, 137

## R

radar
    crew, 86
    operations, 70, 71, 75, 81, 84, 85, 90, 97, 111
    school, 84, 85
    site, 59, 71, 72, 80
radio communications
    fixer net, 71
    VHF/DF transmitters, stations, 70–72
*Rathaus,* 14, 25, 27, 44, 51, 137
refugees, viii, x, 14, 17, 20–22, 29, 30, 53, 56, 58, 59, 90
Regensburg, 20–22
*Regierungsbezirk,* 46, 137, 138
requisitioned housing, forced evictions, 15, 27, 61–64, 68, 136

Rhein-Mann Air Force base, 95
Roman ruins, 20, 21
Romania, 58
Rotterdam, 108
Rügenwalde, 7

## S

Saxony, 12, 14, 16
Schleiger, Eugene R., 1st Lt., 27, 33, 35, 37, 38, 43
School of the Soldier, 102
*SS Washington,* 105
Social Democrat political party, 52
Soviet Union (Soviets, Russians, Red Army), xi, xvi, 3, 11–13,
    15-17, 19, 32, 39, 46, 54, 58, 59, 75, 79, 80, 83, 86, 90, 94, 97,
    99, 101, 103, 107, 109, 131, 132, 133
    censorship of East Germans, 75
    exporting communism, 81
    harassment of Allied planes, 131, 132
    war reparations, 59
Spaatz, Carl A., Gen., xv
Stalag XIIIB, 21
strafing of civilians, 13
Sudetenland, 17

## T

Thalheim, 12–16, 21, 22, 35, 77
*The Task Force Times,* 130
Tilly's relatives, correspondence with
    cousin Clara in California, 75, 77, 78
    cousin Gladys in California, 79
    grandparents in Vienna, 3, 12, 65, 79
    great aunt Luise in Leipzig, 75, 78, 79
    mother Grete in Berlin, Austria, 2–4, 8, 9, 11, 14, 19, 58, 105
    sister Christel in Berlin, Austria, 3, 4, 9, 11, 12, 14, 19, 58, 98
    stepfather Paul in Berlin, 3, 11
    uncle in Vienna, 105
*Trümmerfrauen,* 61, 138
Truman, Harry S., Pres., 15, 45
Tunner, William H., Maj. Gen., 95

## U

Ukrainian refugees, 22
U.S. Air Force (USAF), 81, 83, 89, 94, 95, 132
    604th Aircraft Control and Warning Squadron, 99–103, 105, 124
    7402nd Aircraft Control and Warning Group, 99
U.S. Army Units
    20th Corps, 26, 33, 42
    71st Division, 22
    83rd Armored Reconnaissance Battalion, 14
    90th Division, 17
    115th Cavalry Group, 26
    Counter Intelligence Corps (CIC), 27, 28
U.S. Army Air Corps Commanders of the 604th
    Collins, Fred J., Lt. Col., 95, 96, 101
    Cunningham, Bob, Lt. Col., 67, 74
    McCary, James G., Maj., 87, 101, 103
    McCormick, Jr., Wm A., Maj., 67, 69
    Urquhart, Lloyd C.E., Maj., 83, 84
U.S. Army Air Corps Controllers of the 604th
    Apone, Nicholas R., Lt., 74
    Bell, Frank A., Lt., 63, 73, 74
    Browning, Lt., 63, 74, 87
    Busher, George J., Capt., 63, 73, 74, 87, 91
    Byars, Lt., 73, 74
    Byrne, Charles E., 1st Lt., 84, 91, 95
    Chappell, Orten H., Lt., 74
    Coil, Orville D., Lt., 95, 96
    Cox, George A., 1st Lt., 84, 85, 87, 88, 92, 95, 99
    Davenport, Grady F., 1st Lt., 84, 86–89
    Eastham, James D., 1st Lt., 84, 87–89, 91, 92, 96–98, 101, 129, 132
    Farriss, Lt., 67, 73, 74
    Fuessel, Jr., Aloys W., Capt., 95, 96
    Green, 1st Lt., 75
    Haan, Roger, 2nd Lt., 67, 73
    Hamilton, Lt., 84
    Hansen, Paul H., Lt., 101
    Hearn, Lura E., Lt., 84

Honeywell, John T., 1st Lt., 84
Jutz, Alvin N., Lt., 74
Kapnick, Doc, Lt., 84
Kavanaugh, Jack, 1st Lt., 73
Quilter, Matthew J., 1st Lt., 84, 87, 91, 92, 95
Reas, Capt., 74
Reynolds, Mike "Ralph," Lt., 101
Schlabs, Frank W., Capt., 95, 96
Smith, Kenneth, Lt., 74
Thompson, Lt., 74
van Cleave, Dale, 2nd Lt., 73, 74

U.S. Army Air Corps Units
- 501st Tactical Control Group, 70, 71, 80
- 601st Tactical Control Squadron, 70
- 602nd Tactical Control Squadron, 70
- 603rd Tactical Control Squadron, 70, 80, 90
- 604th Tactical Control Squadron, viii, 59, 61–64, 67, 68, 70–73, 75, 83, 84–86, 89, 90, 91, 95, 98, 136

U.S. Army Air Forces (USAAF), xv, 110-112

U.S. Army Air Forces Units
- 8th Air Force, xv–xvii, 110
- 12th Air Force, 70
- 31st Fighter Group, 89
- 36th Fighter Group, 101
- 51st Troop Carrier Wing, 80
- 55th Fighter Group, 89, 96
- 60th Troop Carrier Group, 96, 130-131
- 100th bombardment group, 109, 112
- 653rd squadron, xvii

U.S. Army Signal Corps Units
- 555th Signal Aircraft Warning Battalion, 70

U.S. Military Government, governance
- Commanders
  - Cochrane, Kenneth S., Capt., 43–45, 48, 49, 53, 57, 58
  - Nordgren, Joseph F., Capt., 118, 121
  - Snow, Albert G., Capt., 23
- field detachments, 46, 47, 138
- Freising Detachment G-231 Special Branch, Company E, 3rd Military Government Regiment, viii, 27, 43, 48, 52, 54

    German resentment against, 29, 49, 56, 62
    Intelligence Division, 56, 118, 151
U.S. Regulations/Acts
    Army Field Manual 27-5, 47
    Army Handbook G-3, 38
    Law Number 8 (see denazification)
    National Security Act of 1947, 81, 126
    War Brides Act of 1945, 43
U.S. Strategic Air Forces in Europe (USSTAF), 80

## V

Victory in Europe (VE) Day, 15, 26
Vienna, 3, 11, 65, 79, 105
*Volksgemeinschaft,* 8, 138
*Volksdeutsche,* 17, 138 (see also expellee)

## W

Weiden in der Oberplatz, 20
Weihenstephan Agricultural and Technical School for American
    Soldiers, viii, 26, 27, 33, 42, 116
Wiesbaden Air Force Base, 80, 95, 96, 99
women's role in
    building German society through childbearing, 2, 104
    food production, acquisition, preparation, 5–7

## Y

Yugoslavia, 58

## Z

Zugspitze, 40, 41, 119

# Questions and Topics for Discussion

1. What was the Nazi ideology regarding the role of Aryan women in the Third Reich? What measures did the regime take to influence the beliefs, values, and actions of girls and women? What characteristics did Tilly possess that did not align with the Nazi's patriarchal mission?

2. What strategies did Tilly employ, and what qualities did she possess that helped her survive the traumas of the war and plan for a postwar future?

3. Why was denazification a priority for the military government? What steps did the military government take to purge Nazi ideology from German society? Why did the scope and intent of denazification become problematic?

4. What made it challenging for Freising to integrate dislocated civilians into their community after the war? In what ways could marginalizing certain members of the community and discouraging their inclusion impede the democratic process? How did Tilly respond to the resentment expressed by residents?

5. A commander of the military government warned the Intelligence Division that the dire circumstances he observed in the community could jeopardize the military government's efforts to promote democratization in Western Germany. He

was particularly concerned about the rise of another demagogue who could exploit the people's underlying attitudes. What were the dire circumstances the commander observed in the community, and what underlying attitudes did he fear could be ignited in the population by a demagogue? Were there similarities in postwar Germany that echoed the conditions contributing to the rise of the Nazi Party in the 1930s? Are there similar challenging situations today that could potentially attract people to a demagogue?

6. After reading about Tilly's experiences working for the American occupation forces in Freising from 1945 to 1949, what conclusions can you draw about how her relationships with the Americans influenced her? How would you describe the interactions between the Americans and the local residents?

7. How did the notion of American democracy gradually seep into German society? What incidents and factors contributed to Tilly's acceptance of American democratic ideals?

8. The German people experienced severe hunger during the war and in the early postwar period, particularly those living in urban areas. What factors contributed to the scarcity of food during this time? What consequences did hunger have on the decisions and actions of Tilly and her family? What was the Allied response to the hunger crisis?

9. Tilly chronicled her world and the people around her through art and photography. In what ways do her images

enhance your understanding of her experiences and those of the American military men assigned to occupy Freising?

10. What insights have you gained from reading about the war and American occupation from Tilly's perspective?

# *About the Author*

Margaret F. Merritt, Ph.D. is a retired research biologist and adjunct assistant professor who has published in the scientific literature and currently enjoys writing historical biographies. She writes to entertain, inform, and inspire reflections on historical issues that remain relevant today. She is the author of *Adventures of an Alaskan Woman Biologist* and *Roshier H. Creecy: A Black Man's Search for Freedom and Prosperity in the Koyukuk Gold Fields of Alaska.* Her book, *Finding Democracy Through the Lens of a Young German Woman, 1944–1950*, is about her mother. Dr. Merritt lives in Alaska.

www.ingramcontent.com/pod-product-compliance
Lightning Source LLC
Chambersburg PA
CBHW051903090426

42811CB00003B/441